SMOKIN'
with
MYRON MIXON

SMOKIN'
with
MYRON MIXON

Recipes Made Simple,
from the
Winningest Man
in Barbecue

Myron Mixon

with Kelly Alexander

Foreword by Paula Deen

Published in the United States by Ballantine Books, an imprint of
The Random House Publishing Group, a division of Random House, Inc., New York.

BALLANTINE and colophon are registered trademarks of Random House, Inc.

Photographs on pages 5, 12, 24, and 56 are by Tom Rankin,
copyright © by Tom Rankin. Used by permission.

Photographs on pages xiii, xiv (bottom), xvi (top), 102, and 109 are from
the author's collection and are reprinted here courtesy of Myron Mixon.

All remaining photographs are by Alex Martinez,
copyright © 2011 by Alex Martinez. Used by permission.

ISBN 978-0-345-52853-7
eISBN 978-0-345-52854-4

Printed in the United States of America on acid-free paper

www.ballantinebooks.com

7 9 8

Book design by Susan Turner

I dedicate this book to my dad, Jack Mixon, for teaching me how to do a lot of things, including barbecuing; and to Pat Burke, for showing me how to be a champion.

CONTENTS

Foreword xi
by Paula Deen

Introduction xiii

1

Barbecue Basics 3

2

Rubs, Sauces, Marinades, Injections, and Glazes 15

Basic Chicken Rub 20

Beef Rub 20

Basic Barbecue Rub 20

Hog Injection 21

Beef Injection and Marinade 21

Rib Marinade 21

Basic Hickory Sauce 22

Basic Vinegar Sauce 22

Chicken Sauce and Glaze 23

Hog Glaze 23

Tangy Sweet Sauce 23

3

Chicken 25

Myron Mixon's World-Famous Cupcake Chicken 29

Old-fashioned Barbecue Chicken 31

Chicken Wings—Two Ways 32

Buffalo Wings   32

Barbecue Wings   33

Wishbone Chicken   36

Bacon-Wrapped Coca-Cola Chicken Breasts   39

Whole Chicken   40

Apple and Bacon–Stuffed Chicken Breasts   42

Smoked Turkey   43

Myron's Signature Buttermilk Fried Chicken   45

4

Hog   47

Whole Hog   53

Pork Shoulder   57

Cracklin' Skins   60

Smoked Jack Bologna   61

Sausage—Two Ways   62

Grilled Sausage   62

Redneck Sausage Hors d'Oeuvres   63

Pork Burgers   64

Pork Loin   65

Stuffed Pork Tenderloin   67

5

Ribs and Chops   69

Rib Spritz   73

St. Louis Ribs   76

Baby Back Ribs   79

Beef Ribs   81

Sausage-Stuffed Pork Chops   84

Rack of Lamb   85

6

Beef   87

Perfect Brisket   90

Perfect Porterhouse Steak   95

Prime Rib   96

Beef Tenderloin   97

Myron Mixon's Prize-Winning Whistler Burger   98

7

Fish   101

Mullet   103

Lobster   105

Salmon   106

Prawns   108

Trout   109

8

Side Dishes   111

Myron's Peach Baked Beans   114

Zesty Potato Salad   116

Mama's Slaw   119

Cracklin' Cornbread   120

Layered Salad with Potato Sticks   121

Brunswick Stew   122

Stuffed Pear Salad   123

Barbecue Deviled Eggs   125

9
Myron at Home   127

Bacon-Wrapped Chicken Livers   129

Lamb Shoulder   130

Fried Catfish   131

Lowcountry Boil   133

Catfish-Shrimp Alfredo   134

Meat Loaf   136

Barbecue Nachos   139

Barbecue-Stuffed Baked Potatoes   140

Chicken Salad   143

Barbecue Chef Salad   144

Pimiento Cheese   145

10
Drinks and Desserts   147

Real Southern Sweet Tea   149

Peachtree Crown Royal Cocktail   151

Jenkins Punch   152

Banana Pudding   155

Apple Crunch   156

Grilled Peaches with Apricot Glaze   157

Acknowledgments   161

Index   164

Foreword

Do y'all recall what it's like to meet a kindred spirit? I'm talking about someone you feel an instant connection to even though you don't really know each other—someone who has walked down the same path you have and lived to tell the tale, so to speak.

That's sorta how I feel about Myron Mixon. Now, I like a man who has the guts to call himself "the winningest son-of-a-bitch in barbecue," but there's more to Myron than his bad-boy attitude. Yes, Myron and I both make a living in the culinary arts, and we both laugh a lot, that's true, too.

When it comes to Myron Mixon, what really pulls at me is the fact that he's pure Georgia-born and Georgia-bred, through and through, just like me. He and I both know what it's like to breathe in that sweet Georgia air, scented with magnolias on a perfect springtime day. I grew up in Albany, Georgia, due southwest from Myron's birthplace of Vienna. My best times growing up were at River Bend, my grandmother and granddaddy's little motel. It was there that I learned about food, where I fell in love with it and came to understand that "food" means something beyond the eating of it—it's an expression of friendship and comfort. People from Georgia like me and Myron get that.

In the South, we're all about traditions, and our traditions have their origins in the cooking pots and the recipes we pass down from generation to generation, like a good cast-iron skillet. I hold these recipes close to my heart. And that's what I like best about Myron Mixon: He learned how to barbecue at his own daddy's knee. He is steeped in these Southern food traditions as thoroughly as I am, and they mean everything to him. There isn't a recipe in this book that isn't a part of his life, a part of his heart, and that's the mark of a truly good cook.

So, what I'm telling y'all is that if you like good barbecue, and I mean the kind of barbecue that you can learn how to make only if you know how to live it, you've come to the right place. And you know the thing about Myron that I like best of all? Like me, he knows that life ain't all about cookin'. It's about enjoying good food with good friends and having a good time. So fire up your smoker, grab a glass of sweet tea, and go make you some of Myron's 'cue.

—PAULA DEEN

Introduction

WHO IS MYRON MIXON?

Here's what you need to know: I am Myron Mixon, from Unadilla, Georgia, and I am the baddest barbecuing bastard there has ever been. As a three-time world barbecue champion, I've been dubbed "The King," "The Best Hog Cooker in the World," "The Man in Black," and more nicknames than I can count—some nice and some downright vicious. No matter what you call me, there's no denying the fact that I'm a fierce competitor and the winningest man in barbecue.

I wasn't always top dog. Not by a long shot. I started out as a small-town operator working at my dad's sawmill and moving from one hard-ass job to another. But I had been raised by Jack Mixon, which, if you're from one of the ten counties that make up middle Georgia, means one thing: barbecue. Folks who knew my dad when he was young remember his shiny black hair and his take-no-prisoners attitude; he got noticed when he went places because he was tall and tough and he always drove the fastest cars (which I later found out was to stay ahead of the

Jack Mixon at his fire pits. In the football jersey is my best friend from school, John Evans, and that's me on the left.

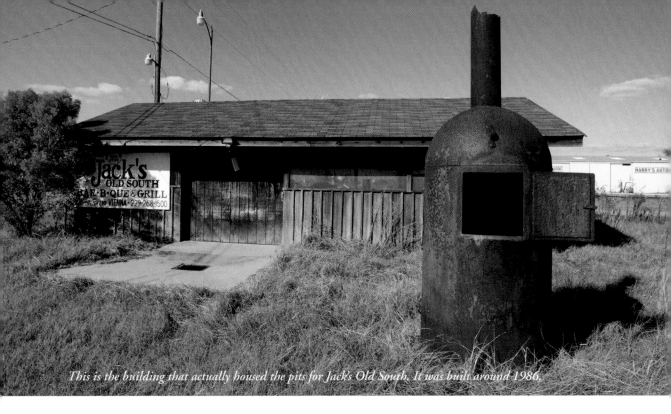

This is the building that actually housed the pits for Jack's Old South. It was built around 1986,

revenuers, but that's a story for another book). Primarily, what my dad did was own a barbecue take-out business in my hometown, Vienna (pronounced VI-anna). Now, my ancestors may have come to this country in the 1600s, but my dad was about as salt-of-the-earth, as honest, and as hardworking a man as you're ever likely to meet. He was also tough

I'm just a simple country boy: one mama, one daddy.

as nails. When I was about ten years old, he had me doing grunt work around his barbecue pits: toting wood, firing up pits, loading

fire barrels, and so on. I did stuff that most young'uns never got asked to do. Jack worked me and my brother Tracy like the free labor

That's me and Tony Woodard, one of my first assistants, competing on the circuit around 1997–98.

we were. I once asked to get paid for my work and Daddy said, "You do, you put your feet under my dinner table and sleep under my roof." When other kids were going swimming and having fun, I was stoking fire pits.

Here's one day I'll never forget: I was just about twelve or so, and my dad had me and my brother Tracy in the yard with him. He had these two big old fire barrels that had to be kept filled with coals, which would be used to heat the barbecue pit. It was as much a job to keep those fire barrels filled as it was to shovel the coals into the pit. Every so often, my father would get off of the five-gallon bucket he was sitting on and he would walk up to the sheets of tin that we had placed across the top of the pits. He would run his hand—no probes or thermometers, just his bare hand—across the tin and then he would tell us to get off our asses and fire those pits. There were three big sections and we had to tend to them about every twenty minutes, or less. The shovels we used were about ten feet long and had steel handles. When they slid into the fire barrel, they'd get so damn hot. The heat was something fierce. My brother and I were trying to do our job, but we were mostly trying to keep ourselves from burning up. It sure wasn't pleasant work, and we did it over and over, all day.

My dad was pretty damn tough on us. People think I'm hard, but they don't have a clue. Sometimes folks who knew my dad because of his barbecue still come up to me and

How Much Have I Won?

Here's why you ought to pay attention to what I say: Since 1996, I've won more than 180 grand championships, 30 state championships (including wins in Georgia, Florida, Alabama, Virginia, Arkansas, Mississippi, Kentucky, Illinois, South Carolina, and Tennessee), and 11 national championships, and I've earned more than 1,800 total trophies. My team has also taken three first-place whole-hog awards at the Jack Daniel's World Championship Invitational Barbecue competition, and we have been crowned the grand champion at the World Championship in Memphis three times (2001, 2004, and 2007). We have also taken first place in the whole-hog category at the World Championship four times (2001, 2003, 2004, and 2007). Jack's Old South has been the Memphis in May Team of the Year with the highest number of points for eight years (from 1999 through 2004, and also in 2007 and 2009). We are also the only team to win grand championships in the Memphis in May, Kansas City BBQ Society, and Florida BBQ Association contests in the same year.

The Jack's Old South team collecting our paychecks at the 2001 Memphis in May World BBQ Championship—my first of three world titles.

ask if Jack is around. I tell them no, he ain't, and you better be damn glad he ain't. He was just a hard man, and a strict father. But he made me who I am; he was someone who could do anything he set his mind to.

Without a doubt, the raising he gave me is what drove me to be able to do what I've done. He schooled me on discipline, determination, and hard work, but what he really taught me

What I do best is beat everybody else's ass.

was how to win. Even when I was a kid trying to keep from burning my hands off, I couldn't help but pay attention to what my dad told me—mostly because I didn't want to have to do anything twice. I learned about the whys and wherefores of barbecue the way the sons of farmers learn to grow crops. It became a

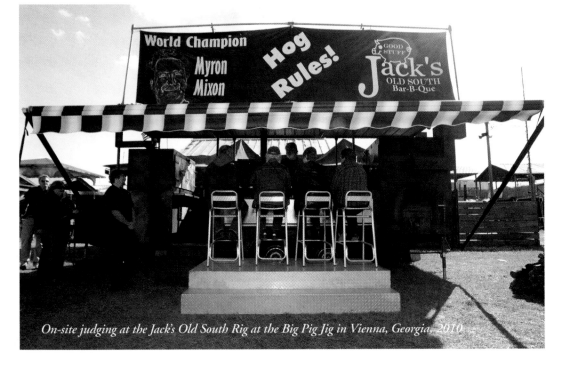

On-site judging at the Jack's Old South Rig at the Big Pig Jig in Vienna, Georgia, 2010.

Myron's Rules to Live By

Now that you know a thing or two about me, let me give you some advice before you strike that match.

It May Be Called Barbecue, but It's Hard Work. This is something I learned in competition that you can apply at home right now: If you don't take cooking seriously, you're not going to make anything tasty. A barbecue might seem like the best place to just sit back and enjoy some good food and drinks, but if you don't respect the fact that there's a right way to do this, your food is never going to come out right.

It's Not About Making Friends. I understand the camaraderie at the barbecue events, and the fact that folks are looking forward to driving up in their motor homes and getting into their little circles and having their little cocktails. There is nothing in the world wrong with that. But that is not what I'm about. If I want to get drunk and have my friends over, I do it on my patio beside my pool. I don't have to spend two grand on ingredients and travel costs and all the rest of the contest expenses to do it. You know what I'm saying? Now, I've been as messed up as a football bat, but that's been after a competition is over and I'm chilling out. Because you can't win the party on Friday night and win the contest on Saturday: It does not work like that. So when you're cooking, pay attention to what you're doing.

Stay Cool. Some people get all in a tizzy over all their stuff, the dishes they're making, all of it coming together at the same time. Well, guess what? That's what cooking's about. You've got to figure out a timetable for yourself. And you've got to keep a level head. You can get everything ready to go on time if you keep it calm and organized, and I'll show you how.

Never a Dull Moment. When you present your barbecue to the judges at a Memphis in May event, you have to put on a show. You don't want a lot of quiet time because you don't want the judge thinking; you want his happy ass eating. My food is what wins. The presentation is just a floor show that you enjoy your meal by. That said, when people come to Jack's Old South, they expect and they want the dog and pony show. When people come over to your house, don't just sling the food at them. Let them see you work. Let them see that you know what you're doing. Then go have some drinks around the pool and relax.

part of me, a part of my way of thinking, and I didn't even know it was happening. I didn't realize it for a long time, actually—not until my father had a stroke and passed away unexpectedly in January of 1996. Until then, I didn't want anything to do with barbecue.

It surprises people when they find out that my first feelings about barbecue were so bad. So how did things turn around? I'll tell

It's good to be the king.

you. By the mid-1990s, I had two boys of my own and was living a life that had nothing to do with barbecue. At the same time, my parents had started making and selling their own barbecue sauce from a recipe that came from my mother's side of the family. They were fairly successful with it and it was a nice side business for them, but it didn't much concern me. When my father died, though, I started thinking about how I could help my family and continue my father's legacy. At that point, I was focused on the sauce. It was a great sauce, but for it to sell, I knew that I needed to find a way to publicize it.

There is an important barbecue contest in Vienna, Georgia, called the Big Pig Jig. It began small in 1982, but it became an enormous event, with on-site professional barbecue judging and more than $20,000 in prize money. That event got me to thinking of entering some barbecue competitions to

Big Pig Jig in Vienna, Georgia, 2010

That's me at home with my big white bulldog, Jack.

promote our family's barbecue sauce. So just six months after my father passed away and with absolutely no professional barbecue experience (but plenty of confidence), I entered my first contest, the Lock-&-Dam BBQ Contest in Augusta, Georgia. To everyone's surprise but my own, I took first place in the whole-hog category, first place in the ribs category, and third place in the pork shoulder category. Did I mention it was my very first contest?

After that, the sauce became a sideline for me, too. Once I got a taste of how successful I could be at competitive barbecue, I became single-minded in my devotion to it. I was going to become the champion of this universe, or die trying. I just kept pushing myself to create the best barbecue I could, and I kept winning and winning. Since then, I've won more barbecue competitions than anyone else and have earned more than $1,000,000 in prize money. I've got rooms in my house just for the trophies.

My professional life is on the competitive barbecue circuit and I have no intention of ever giving it up. I want to continue to win because I never want to give up the title of the winningest man in barbecue, and if someone wants to take my throne, they're going to have to work their ass off to snag it from me. But some interesting things have happened along the way. As a result of all of my success at the various contests, I attracted the attention of a serious barbecue enthusiast who happened to also be a multi–Emmy award-winning television producer named John Markus. He wanted to work with me on some sort of barbecue show because he knew there was no one better to approach. So he taped me in my element, both at home

and at contests, and pitched his ten-minute barbecue documentary to television studios. And that's how the TLC network show that I'm on, *BBQ Pitmasters,* got its start.

Well, let me tell you: The success of the show is nice and I get a kick out of doing those appearances, but I don't for a second think it means I can stop tending the smoker

> **When it comes to Myron Mixon cooking whole hog . . . well, that's just like spitting off a damn train, that's just how easy it is for me.**

and sit around the pool sipping daiquiris. In fact, nowadays I have to work twice as hard because my competitors have seen my recipes and techniques on television. But from the response to the show and my experience teaching a barbecue school (ten weekends a year in what I like to call the "House That 'Cue Built," a brick-and-mortar temple to barbecue erected at my home), I've come to realize how much home cooks would like to learn about how to make good barbecue, and I've realized how the things I do in competition can easily be adapted to what you do when you're cooking in your backyard.

No disrespect to my fellow barbecue professionals, but I don't think the world needs another barbecue book that home cooks can't and won't use. I'm going to give you lessons on how to cook barbecue that will win, whether you plan to compete at a contest or just want to impress your friends and neighbors on the Fourth of July. I'm sharing my best stories from the front lines of the barbecue circuit, and I'm going to provide barbecue recipes, tips, and advice that you'll really be able to use. Once I show you exactly how to make my barbecue, you won't ever need to try any other way again. And I'm not just blowing smoke.

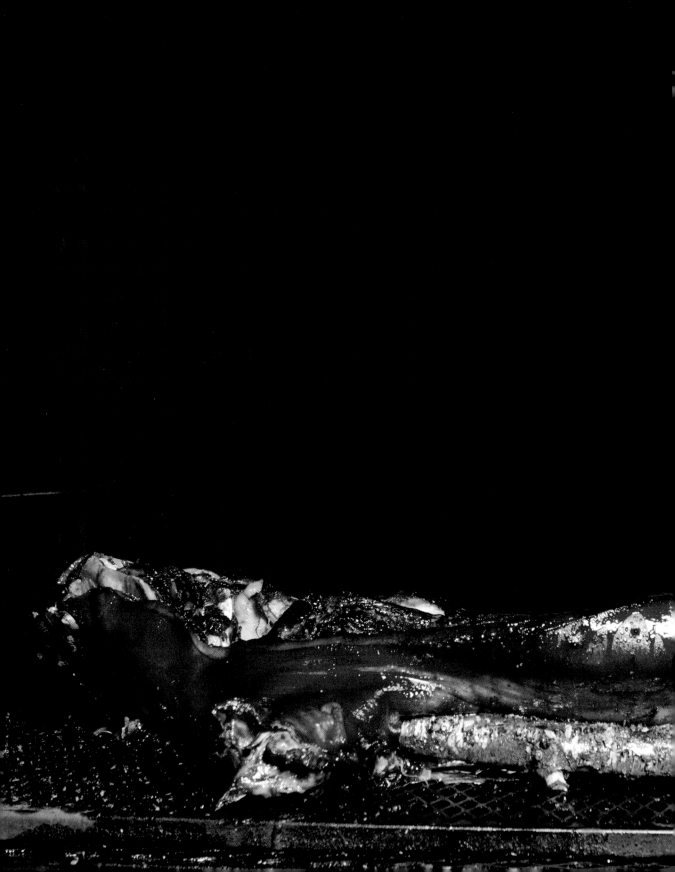

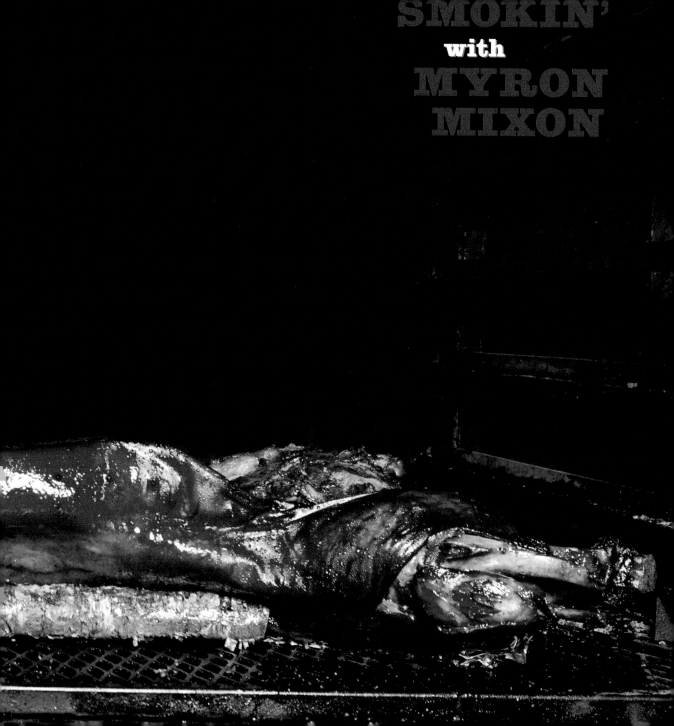

SMOKIN'
with
MYRON
MIXON

Barbecue Basics

Men like to barbecue. Men will cook if danger is involved.
—Rita Rudner

A FUNNY THING HAPPENS when I get to competitions: I find myself surrounded by lots of "friends" who show up at opportune times, like when I'm prepping my meat. These are people who want to watch me cook, see what I do, and figure out what techniques they can steal for their own food. I'm not ugly to them. In fact, I'm fine with their prying eyes because I know that no matter what they see me doing, they're probably not going to be able to replicate the magic themselves. That's not because I think I'm so divine—although of course I do think that—but it's because there's just no substitute for the amount of practice I've had. I've spent a lifetime growing up around barbecue, and I'm closing in on twenty years of competing on the professional barbecue circuit. So watch all you like, I say: You won't be able to do what I do unless you put in the time.

Now, that said, I do appreciate the fact that people admire my food and want to learn some of my tricks. It's flattering. And I like to help teams, especially the young ones just getting started who really want to learn, and so I figured out something I could do besides watch them all turn into eavesdropping fools. For a few years now I've been running a barbecue cooking school in my backyard barbecue pavilion, where I've set up an outdoor classroom. My students come for a weekend and learn how to do what I do in competition; they watch as I demonstrate how to cook all the major categories of barbecue meats, and they get the opportunity to work in teams and make their own. I attract a wide variety of students, from people who just want to learn how to make their barbecues better, to those who are interested in learning to cook on the circuit, to barbecue restaurant owners hoping to shoot some extra energy into their menu offerings.

I have a lot of fun teaching, and to be honest with you, I wish my students would have a little more fun. I notice a whole lot of worriation among my pupils. They stress over cooking times and temperatures. If I say "Sprinkle some rub on the brisket," they want to know *exactly* how much to sprinkle on; if I say "Let the chicken rest a few minutes," they want to know *exactly* how many minutes. I think you have to be very mindful of times and temperatures when you're cooking, and you have to set a timeline and be vigilant about sticking to it. Lord knows I'm sometimes a slave to my timelines, which I spend a lot of time devising, during competitions. But I also believe that it's just as important to use your other senses when you're cooking, too. For instance, I often go by appearance when I'm cooking: Does my meat have the color on it that I want it to? Is

it that just-right shade of burnished yet shiny? I want my food to look great, and getting the color I want on it lets me know when it's ready. My philosophy: It's done when it's done, and when it's done, get it off the grill.

Again, that kind of judgment comes with a lot of practice. You'll get there, but you have to start somewhere. So I figure that this is a good place to tackle your most worrisome questions about barbecue. Without further ado, here are the top questions that people ask me about how to cook barbecue—with my answers.

What is barbecue supposed to taste like?

If we're talking about championship barbecue here, the first thing you have to remember is that all barbecue contests are meat contests. And so no matter what, the essential flavor of the meat should come through. This rule is equally true for what you cook up in your own backyard. Beyond that, good barbecue should obviously be moist and tender,

but it should also have layers of flavor that are balanced and that cooperate with one another in your mouth. So the first layer of this is the natural flavor of the meat you're cooking. On top of that are the flavors it picks up from the marinade and rub you apply and the sauce you finish the meat with. Finally, and just as important, is the flavor of the smoke that enters the meat. Because at the end of the day, smoke is what makes barbecue.

What is the difference between grilling and barbecuing?

The fact that there's confusion over the exact differences between grilling and barbecuing

Myron's Tip

DON'T OPEN YOUR SMOKER IF YOU DON'T HAVE TO. Why? Because every time you open it, you lower the temperature inside it by about 5 degrees or so. It'll take several additional minutes of cooking time to make up for that loss of heat. And when you're cooking barbecue, it's very important to maintain a consistent temperature in the smoker.

shows me that people really like to cook outside, but they sure need a little more knowledge—because anything you cook on a grill is not necessarily "barbecue." Grilling is cooking food fast and at high heat: 350° to 400°F and up. Think of it this way: It's the perfect way to sear a steak, because grilling is great for meat that is already relatively tender. Barbecuing is an altogether different process: It's cooking over a low (or indirect) fire with a heat that's 350°F or lower, and it involves smoking. When you barbecue, you want to not only cook the meat but also infuse and tenderize it with the smoke and the flavors coming from the wood. A little tip to remember: You can barbecue anything that you can grill, but you can't grill everything that you can barbecue. You can barbecue and grill chicken breasts, for instance, but you wouldn't want to grill a big tough cut of meat like a beef brisket.

What's the best barbecue cooker?

Let me demystify this for you: To make delicious barbecue, there is no requirement that you must have high-end equipment like I use in competitions. Barbecue came about because there was a need for people to be able to feed themselves simply and cheaply. With the right recipes and an understanding of time, temperature, and flavor, you can achieve tasty food on any type of smoker, whether store-bought or homemade. The best barbecue cooker for you is the one that you feel most comfortable using. When choosing a cooker, there are a few things to consider: price range, what size meats you'll want to cook and what quantities you'll want to use, and, most important, your level of expertise. It is easier to learn on simple equipment and then move on to more advanced types of cookers than it is to jump headfirst into top-tier smokers and try to figure it out from there.

Now, most American households own a grill or smoker. The majority of these are grills fueled by propane gas—they're by far the most popular choice. On their own, gas grills don't give off that smoky flavor we who love barbecue crave, but they can be adapted so that they do. Regular kettle grills, like the much-loved Webers, also have capability for smoking. As far as smokers go, there's an incredible range, from the charcoal "bullet" smokers to rigs like the ones that I have custom-built. There are also Asian-inspired ceramic cookers, like the Big Green Egg, which have an army of enthusiasts. To my way of thinking, your cooker is your cooker; I can help you adapt any of them to properly smoke food. The most important thing, far more important than what style of cooker you use, is the mastery of proper barbecue cooking techniques.

Can I smoke food on a gas grill?

You bet your ass you can. Most of the models of gas grills have either two or three burners

One of my many smokers, this one is called the "Little Jack."

that can be controlled individually. Here's what to do: Take your favorite wood chips and soak them in water overnight. Drain them, wrap them in foil, and then poke several holes in the top of the packet. Set the packet of chips aside. On a two-burner gas grill, light only one side; on a three-burner unit, light the two outside burners and leave the middle one cold. Place your packet of wood chips on the lit section (or sections). The flame will smolder the wet chips, producing smoke for your meat. To smoke on a gas grill, place your meat on the unlit section. That's it. (Don't worry about the side vents and making them closed airtight; do the best you can to shut them, but none of my smokers are airtight, either. All my methods are simple, so let's not worry so much and make them complicated, all right?)

How Smoking Got Started

You have to remember that smoking meat is a very old process. It began in the days long before refrigeration, when farmers and butchers had to take extra or unsold meat and figure out how to not let it go to waste. Meat markets and farmers would smoke the meat. Along the way, they figured out how to make it taste good by placing emphasis on the quality of the meat, the seasoning, and the wood. Barbecue is a really humble food, and it drives me crazy when people forget that. It takes time and attention and care, but it is surely not something beyond anyone's imagination. It's as down-to-earth as it can be.

Can I smoke on a kettle grill?

You bet your ass you can. Soak your wood chips or chunks in water overnight. Drain them. Set them aside. On a regular kettle grill, you need to bank your charcoal to one side, leaving a cold area for the meat to be placed. Put the wood chips directly on your coals. Place the lid on the kettle and control the heat with the dampers (vents). Now you're really barbecuing.

What kind of wood should I use?

I like fruit woods because they're mild in flavor, high in sap, and have fewer impurities in them. When you cook with hickory and oak, which have more impurities in them, the impurities get on the grill, and if they get on the grill, then where else are they? That's right: in your food. This doesn't happen with milder and purer fruit woods. And note that when I say "mild," I'm meaning it as a compliment:

There are a lot of flavor components on my meat, from rubs to marinades to glazes, and I look to the wood to add the most important base coat of smoke and subtle flavor but not to dominate the entire piece of meat. Make sense? Good. Now, if you have any access to dry fruit woods, take advantage of it. Because I live in Georgia, I have great access to peach wood, and that's what I've used since I started competitive barbecue cooking. But if you can get your hands on apple wood, pear wood, apricot wood, grapevine wood, or cherry wood, I say have at it—any

and all of these are my top choices for the best barbecue.

What are the essential items to have in your barbecue pantry?

Since I started competing in 1996, all my ingredients have been items that can be picked up at the local supermarket. I am not into fancy ingredients; I'm into things that are tried-and-true, items that I know will taste good. That said, you can buy whichever brand, from the fanciest gourmet version to the house brand at any supermarket, and if you follow my recipes and combine them the way I tell you to, your barbecue will turn out delicious. So these are the things I always have on hand:

Ketchup

Light brown sugar

Dark brown sugar

Maple syrup

Light corn syrup

Apple juice

Distilled white vinegar

Salt

Sugar

Hot sauce (I've experimented a lot and prefer the Cajun Louisiana brand, chiefly because it's thin enough to fit through the injection syringe)

Apple jelly

Blackberry preserves

Peach preserves

Ac'cent flavor enhancer (also known as MSG, or monosodium glutamate; if you're philosophically opposed to this, try out some of those "Cajun spice blends" in the spice department of your supermarket)

Imitation butter flavoring

Chicken broth

Beef broth concentrate (I like Minor's brand, which is available via mail order from soupbase.com; if you can't find it, you can substitute some very strong beef stock)

Jack's Old South Vinegar Sauce (this comes from me—it's my own brand of barbecue sauce and is available at jacksoldsouth.com; if you must, substitute a favorite brand)

Jack's Old South Hickory Sauce (this is my own brand, too, so sue me)

A Note on Aluminum Foil and Pans

Some folks in the world of barbecue look down their noses at cooks like me who use aluminum foil to wrap meats and who put meat in aluminum pans. The reason is because they don't feel it's authentic; because, you know, cavemen at the beginning of time didn't do it this way. So what is my answer? The reason I use aluminum pans is because they present the easiest way to handle meat. They keep the meat from falling apart, which you risk when you transfer it from a prep station to a smoker, and using an aluminum pan makes cleanup a whole lot easier. Bottom line: You don't want your meat falling apart, and you don't want to have to spend your days constantly scraping down your grill.

Why do you put a pan of water in your smoker?

I get so many questions about this, and honestly I wish I didn't. What I preach about barbecue is that it's simple and easy, and so I tell folks to stop trying to make it complicated. Besides, the issue of my water pan really seems to confuse people. They just don't get why I use it. But if you insist, here's the deal: A water pan is not a requirement to cook barbecue. However, it does have a significant benefit. What it does is create a water bath system inside the smoker that helps maintain the meat's moisture content, which is found naturally in the fat, or marbling, of the meat. So the water pan doesn't so much infuse the meat with moisture as it helps maintain what's already in there. It tenderizes the meat while you're barbecuing it, and that's a good thing. If you'd like to try the method, simply fill a heavy-bottomed medium-size pan (no bigger than a simple 13 × 9-inch lasagna pan) about halfway with water and place it in

the bottom of your smoker and see how it works for you.

Why do you let meat rest after you cook it?

When I take my meat off the smoker—no matter what kind of meat—I make sure I let it rest, gently covered with some aluminum foil, either in the pan I've cooked it in or on a cutting board for at least 20 minutes and sometimes more (in each recipe I give specific rest times; don't worry). Let me tell you: If you do not let the meat rest, it is not going to be worth a damn. It has to rest after you cook

it so that the flavor can come back into it. You've got to let it rest sitting right down in its own juices. It allows the flavors to concentrate, it allows the texture to solidify, and it regulates the temperature throughout the piece of meat. Never skip this step, no matter how much of a hurry you may be in to get your food on the table.

How should I start my fire?

I am a stick-burning competitor. Nothing flavors the meat like whole sticks of wood, which is what barbecue is about—the flavor of natural smoke combined with the right seasonings and sauce. That said, I do start my fire with charcoal just to get a blaze going to burn the wood. And I start the charcoal with lighter fluid under protest and scrutiny from fellow competitors. They imply that the meat will taste like the fluid. Well, that's true if you don't read the damn directions on the bottle and after applying the fluid, let the coals burn white. In other words, all you have to do is burn the fluid off before you put your meat on. Then you've started your fire as easily as possible while still getting the benefit of cooking over real wood.

How do I get my food to look like yours?

When I am in competition, the appearance of my food is serious business. Not only is it a major component of my overall score (and thus how much money I'll make), but it's also very strictly governed by the sanctioning bodies. For instance, at Kansas City Barbecue Society (KCBS) events, entries for judging must be placed in 9 × 9-inch Styrofoam containers that may be garnished with green leaves of lettuce, parsley, or cilantro only. At Memphis in May (MIM) events, the same size Styrofoam box is used, but entries may not be garnished with anything at all—although the boxes may include up to two small cups of sauces, rubs, or marinades

alongside the food. I think a lot about making my food so attractive that one Styrofoam box full of it will look so much better than the dozens and sometimes hundreds of similar boxes that the judges are seeing. I mean, I wake up in the middle of the night and make sketches of how I'm going to build a box.

Late one night before a Memphis in May contest, I couldn't stop thinking about the presentation I would offer up to the judges the next day, so I went to the all-night Denny's across the street from my hotel and stayed up until dawn sketching out my plans for my hog box, and I ended up winning the grand championship that year.

So that shows you how seriously I take the subject of food's appearance. Do you have to take it that seriously? Well, maybe you should. I'm not saying you ought to lose sleep over what the food's going to look like at your kid's family birthday barbecue, but you'll please a whole lot more people if your food looks delicious. Applying some of the lessons I've learned the hard way on the barbecue circuit is good for that. I give tips throughout this book on how to help you get your food looking good—from spritzing ribs to getting bark on brisket—and if you follow my advice, your food will look damn good, too.

Rubs, Sauces, Marinades, Injections, and Glazes

A well-made sauce will make even an elephant or a grandfather palatable.
—Alexandre Balthazar Laurent Grimod de la Reynière

SINCE MAN LIT the first fire for cooking, he has constantly strived for more flavor in his food. It began with seasonings such as salt, sugars, and pepper. How you choose to season your meat is a highly personal decision. That's because we all have different preferences and we all use enhancements, like sauces and rubs and marinades, for one reason: to get great flavor. And by that I mean harmonious flavors, things that seem to belong together. To do this, you have to be willing to experiment. I am always tinkering with my rubs, injections, and glazes to try to make them better and more delicious, and I don't know a competitive barbecue cook out there who isn't.

A rub's job is to season the meat, help seal in moisture, and ensure that you get a nice crust (or "bark," if you will) on your smoked meats. A marinade's or injection's job is to infuse the meat with flavor, tenderize the meat by breaking down the meat's muscle fibers, and keep the meat moist as it cooks. Glazes contain sugar and are best thought of as finishing sauces; they're the final step when the meat is all but fully cooked, and they help lock in a nice moist and tender texture. Sauce is what you put on your meat after it's been cooked. That's a whole layering process right there, and you'll notice that there's plenty of

overlap in the functions of these things. Hey, I never said cooking wasn't a repetitive process.

When you're making something like barbecue, understanding and mastering these processes is the difference between having enough gas money to drive your rig home and not. The trend in barbecue cooking these days is injections. I like injections because they shoot flavors deep into the meat. When a judge comes by at an MIM event, he or she wants to taste the meat that's right next to the bone, deep on the inside of the piece of meat.

A dry rub isn't going to touch that area. I'll be honest with you: When people started cooking barbecue, back at the dawn of time when the first fires were lit, they weren't using syringe-like injections to flavor their meats. And so there's an idea that some people have about injections that they're not "pure" or they're not "authentic," because folks haven't been doing it that way since the beginning of time.

Well, I'll tell you something. I know "authentic" like the best of them. I know about how in ancient times men barbecued out of necessity more than out of desire. Those were the days when barbecuing was a way of life; it wasn't done because of competitions or to be the next food trend—they did it to feed their families, and to do it cheaply. My daddy, Jack Mixon, first taught me barbecuing on an open pit. He lit fires with lightered knots (country boys know that these are knots of wood from old-growth pine trees, one hundred years or older, which are dead and have been dead for ages and thus are almost petrified; these trees had very close growth rings and grew very slowly and were a lot hardier and had more sap and tar than today's varieties, and as a result are highly flammable to the point that some explosives are still made from them). He loaded fire barrels and shoveled coals all night, and when my brother Tracy and I were old enough, we did that, too. We'd stay awake all night, listening to grease sizzling on the embers and inhaling the powerful aromas that filled the air.

I believe there's value in preserving tradition. I believe that it's important to try to revive this method of cooking that's almost forgotten. I even teach a class called "Barbecue Memories" that's devoted to this time-honored cooking style. I take only fifteen students, and it's an intimate experience; we stay up together, sharing knowledge and fellowship, and taking in the scents of my childhood. We cook on the identical replica of my

dad's original masonry pits that I had painstakingly reconstructed in my own backyard. On those occasions, I'm all about open-pit cooking.

But let me tell you something else: That has very little to do with the world of competitive barbecue cooking, and times change. Our concern is still the same—turning out the most delicious meat possible—but staying up all night over an open pit is just completely impractical, whether you're at a competition or in your own backyard. It's

also all but impossible because when we cook in competitions, we have to show up with our meat totally untouched for inspection by judges, so that no one gets an advantage. We can't apply the rubs or marinades to our meat, or inject them, before the contest offi-

I can beat their ass cooking on a trash can.

cially begins. And we have fixed windows of time in which to get everything ready. If you want to stay up all night and stoke a fire pit, you're probably going to lose and you definitely won't have enough time to enter all the categories required for a grand championship

title. If you're throwing a backyard barbecue, pit cooking might sound nice, but doing it my way is far more practical, and that includes using injections.

I don't mind the fact that cooking barbecue has evolved over the centuries. Hell, I embrace it. I'm all about doing whatever it takes to get the desired result to win. In my view, to have the best barbecue you should use whatever you need to in order to produce it. Injections are just the flavor of the week, if you will, and they're mighty effective at getting flavor into the meat. And until something even better comes along, I'm going to stick with my winning techniques. Flavoring food is and will always be a never-ending journey. Let's start yours right here, right now.

Basic Chicken Rub

Makes 2 cups

2/3 cup chili powder
1/2 cup sugar
4 tablespoons kosher salt

4 tablespoons onion powder
4 tablespoons garlic powder
1 teaspoon cayenne pepper

In a large bowl, combine all the ingredients thoroughly. You can store this rub in an airtight container indefinitely.

Beef Rub

Makes about 1/4 cup

1 teaspoon kosher salt
2 tablespoons coarsely ground
   black pepper
1 teaspoon sugar
1/2 teaspoon chipotle pepper
   powder

1/2 teaspoon chili powder
1 teaspoon garlic powder
1 teaspoon granulated dried
   onion

In a large bowl, combine all the ingredients thoroughly. You can store this rub in an airtight container indefinitely.

Basic Barbecue Rub

Makes 3 cups

1 cup (packed) light brown sugar
2 tablespoons chili powder
2 tablespoons dry mustard
2 tablespoons onion powder
2 tablespoons garlic powder

2 tablespoons cayenne pepper
2 tablespoons kosher salt
2 tablespoons coarsely ground
   black pepper

In a large bowl, combine all the ingredients thoroughly. You can store this rub in an airtight container indefinitely.

Hog Injection

Makes 5 quarts

4 quarts apple juice
1 quart distilled white vinegar
5 pounds sugar
2 cups salt

1 cup monosodium glutamate,
    such as Ac′cent brand flavor
    enhancer

In a large stockpot, combine the apple juice and vinegar over medium heat. Stirring continuously, pour in the sugar, salt, and monosodium glutamate. Stir until the seasonings are completely dissolved. Do not boil. Remove from the heat.

If reserving for a later use, let the liquid cool; then pour it into a large bottle or container. Store refrigerated for up to 1 year.

Beef Injection and Marinade

Makes 1 quart

1 quart water
3 tablespoons Minor's brand beef
    base (see Note) or beef
    bouillon powder

3 tablespoons Minor's brand beef
    au jus concentrate (see Note),
    or 1 15-ounce can strong beef
    broth

In a large stockpot over high heat, bring the water to a boil. Add the beef base and the beef au jus to the water, and stir until dissolved. Remove from the heat.

If reserving for a later use, let the liquid cool; then pour it into a jug or bottle. This can be stored in the refrigerator for up to 2 weeks. *Note: Minor's products are available for mail order via soupbase.com.*

Rib Marinade

Makes about 7½ cups

1 liter ginger ale
1 quart orange juice
1¼ cups soy sauce

½ cup salt
2 1-ounce packets dry ranch
    dressing mix

In a large bowl, combine all the ingredients. Stir well to thoroughly incorporate. Pour into a large bottle or other container and store, refrigerated, for up to 2 weeks.

Basic Hickory Sauce

Makes 3½ cups

2 tablespoons onion powder

2 tablespoons garlic powder

2 cups ketchup

2 tablespoons smoked sweet
    paprika

2/3 cup cider vinegar

2 tablespoons Worcestershire sauce

¼ cup (packed) dark brown sugar

2 tablespoons honey

2 tablespoons maple syrup

2 tablespoons kosher salt

2 tablespoons freshly ground
    black pepper

Combine all the ingredients in a blender and pulse until thoroughly combined. Pour into a medium pot, and stir continuously over medium heat until heated through. Do not allow it to boil. Remove and use while hot.

If reserving for a later use, allow the mixture to cool; then pour it into a large bottle or container and store, refrigerated, for up to 1 year.

Basic Vinegar Sauce

Makes about 3½ cups

2 cups cider vinegar

1 cup ketchup

½ cup hot sauce

2 tablespoons salt

2 tablespoons coarsely ground
    black pepper

1 tablespoon red pepper flakes

½ cup sugar

In a stockpot over medium heat, combine the vinegar, ketchup, and hot sauce. Stir together. Pour in all the remaining ingredients and stir to dissolve. Do not boil. When the spices are thoroughly dissolved, take the pot off the heat, and funnel the sauce into a bottle. The sauce will keep, refrigerated, for up to 1 year.

Chicken Sauce and Glaze

Makes about 6 cups

1 cup ketchup
1 cup Jack's Old South Vinegar
  Sauce or Basic Vinegar Sauce
  (page 22)
1 cup Jack's Old South Hickory
  Sauce or Basic Hickory Sauce
  (page 22)

1 cup honey
1 cup maple syrup
1 cup (packed) dark brown sugar
8 tablespoons (1 stick) unsalted
  butter, melted

Pour all the ingredients into a large blender. Combine thoroughly, blending for at least 3 minutes. Pour the mixture into a medium pot and stir constantly over medium heat until the sauce is hot. Do not allow it to boil. Remove from the stove and use while hot.

If you're reserving it for a later use, pour the sauce into a large bottle or other container. Store, refrigerated, for up to 2 months. Always reheat this sauce before using.

Hog Glaze

Makes 8 cups

2 cups Jack's Old South Vinegar
  Sauce or Basic Vinegar Sauce
  (page 22)

2 18-ounce jars apple jelly
2 cups light corn syrup

Combine all the ingredients in a blender, and blend until thoroughly combined, about 3 minutes. Pour out into a clean bowl, using a plastic spatula to scrape it all. Store, refrigerated, for up to 2 weeks.

Tangy Sweet Sauce

Makes about 4 1/3 cups

1 cup Jack's Old South Vinegar
  Sauce or Basic Vinegar Sauce
  (page 22)

1 cup light corn syrup
1 18-ounce jar peach preserves

Combine all the ingredients in a blender, and blend until thoroughly combined. Scrape into a large container or bottle. Store, refrigerated, for up to 1 year.

3

Chicken

Left wing, chicken wing, it don't make no difference to me.
—Woody Guthrie

HOW DO I FEEL about cooking chicken at a barbecue competition? I can sum it up pretty easily: I hate it. It has nothing to do with the way it tastes—I love to eat it. But it's the toughest damn category in competitive barbecue. Comparatively, chicken takes a lot of preparation time and it's just the most tedious work. I can prep all of my other categories, including a whole hog, in less time than it takes me to prep chicken.

Now, the reason it takes so long to prep chicken is primarily because of the way the judging works. In professional competitions, the judges dictate what the teams turn in by the way the scoring is done. For each category, there is an appearance rating for your entry, determined by its visual appeal. So before the judges even taste the food, they've decided if it looks good enough to eat. And their definition of "good enough to eat" is probably not the same as yours or mine. The food can't just look tasty; the judges favor chicken pieces that are absolutely uniform in shape and color. Have you ever tried to get chicken pieces to look identical?

One of the most important things I've learned during the past fifteen years on the circuit is that competitors come and go pretty frequently. That's because it's hard to consistently make great barbecue over a long period of time. On the road, I see a lot of barbecue teams that come into a contest and win for that moment. They do very well, but then they vanish. You see them go away because they keep trying to do what they already did, what won it for them the first time, and that just won't work. To succeed, you can't keep cooking the same food, no matter how good it is. So you have to find a way to keep things fresh. Why? Because too many other people are taking the time and spending the money to improve—whether it be with new equipment, with cooking classes, by reading cookbooks, or by watching cooking videos. You can't be complacent and hope that what you did five years ago will work today. It ain't going to happen. Keeping this in mind was one of the most important factors in overcoming the challenge of chicken at a contest.

The chicken category, more than any other, illustrates how hard I've had to work on my own food and how I keep evolving my techniques. Nowadays I'm famous for my "cupcake chicken," which is a recipe I came up with after years of trying to figure out exactly how to get my chicken not only to taste delicious but also to look perfect. In my backyard I love to cook chicken breasts—wait

until you try the ones I roll up in bacon—and I love wings, which are fun to make and delicious. But in competition, I go with what most competitors do: thighs. The reason is simple: Compared to other parts of the chicken, thighs are easier to trim into similar sizes. There I was, trying to figure out how to get my chicken to look right: How could I get the thighs all the same size? A mold, I thought. So I bought a silicone cupcake mold, just like the kind you'd bake blueberry muffins in, and trimmed my thighs as close to the same dimensions as I could, sizing them up and butchering each piece. And then I placed those thighs in that mold. When they were cooked on the smoker and then unmolded, they looked like they were clones. Mission accomplished.

My cupcake chicken technique solved a lot of problems for me in competition, and made it so that the chicken category has become a much more consistent win for me. I like the method so much that these days I just tinker with my formula: I may change the rub, or the glaze, but I stick with my technique. And at competition I see more and more teams unpack their muffin tins when they set up, and I just laugh. Hell, some local stores near me stock muffin tins in the outdoor cooking department now.

The recipe is useful for home cooks, too: Even when you're cooking out in your back-yard for friends, you're going to want your food to look appealing. And besides looking good, my cupcake chicken is easy to make, and damn tasty. Between the smoking process with which it's cooked and the blackberry-spiked glaze I apply to it, it's moist, deeply flavored, and loaded up with the tastes of smoke and spice and sweetness. I get a mouthwatering dark red, deep mahogany, shiny, lacquered color on each piece every time. And so will you.

To be sure, the chicken recipes in this chapter will not give you the worriation that the competition barbecue chicken category gave me. That's because the plain fact is that chicken is a natural to cook on a smoker or a grill, and it's one of the easiest things to cook. Oftentimes at a barbecue it's everyone's favorite thing to eat, so you really need to have a handful of proven chicken recipes. What I am giving you here is the benefit of all the trial-and-error attempts that I've undertaken in order to figure out how to cook chicken. All my favorite recipes are here, and you should try them all. I guarantee you'll find winning recipes whether you're into wings or breasts or, like me, you go for the whole bird.

Myron Mixon's World-Famous Cupcake Chicken

Makes 12 appetizer or 6 main-course servings

12 medium skin-on, bone-in chicken
   thighs
2 cups Jack's Old South Huney Muney
   Cluck Rub, or 1 recipe Basic Chicken
   Rub (page 20)

3¼ cups chicken broth
Salt, to taste
Freshly ground black pepper, to taste

For the sauce:
1 cup Jack's Old South Vinegar Sauce or
   Basic Vinegar Sauce (page 22)
2 cups Jack's Old South Hickory Sauce
   or Basic Hickory Sauce (page 22)
1 cup ketchup

1 cup honey
1 cup maple syrup
1¼ cups seedless blackberry preserves
8 tablespoons (1 stick) unsalted butter,
   at room temperature

What you'll need:
Poultry shears
1 silicone cupcake mold, with holes
   punched through each cup (or an
   aluminum cupcake pan, also with
   holes punched through each cup)

1 13 × 9-inch aluminum baking pan
1 aluminum baking sheet

Heat a smoker to 300°F.

Using poultry shears, remove the knuckle on each end of each chicken thigh bone. Then trim the excess fat off the skin and meat of each thigh until the pieces are 3 to 4 inches wide, leaving about ¼ inch of excess skin at the edges of the meat. Apply the chicken rub evenly to both sides of the thighs.

In the cupcake mold, place each thigh, skin side down, in an individual cup. Sit the mold in the baking pan, and pour the chicken broth into the pan, being careful not to pour it directly on top of the chicken. Place the pan in the smoker and cook, uncovered, for 1½ hours.

Remove the baking pan from the smoker. Gently flip the thighs onto the baking sheet. Season the tops of the thighs with salt and pepper. Return the thighs to the mold cups, skin side up, and put the baking pan back in the smoker. Cook for 45 minutes.

Meanwhile, make the sauce: Put all the sauce ingredients into a blender and blend until thoroughly combined. In a medium pan over medium heat, warm the sauce until it is hot but not boiling. Set aside.

Remove the pan from the smoker, and unmold the chicken thighs onto the baking sheet, skin side up. Brush the thighs lightly with the warm sauce. Place the baking sheet in the smoker and cook for 30 minutes to allow the sauce to caramelize into the chicken skin.

Remove the baking sheet from the smoker, and serve the cupcake chicken immediately.

Old-fashioned Barbecue Chicken

Some folks hear "barbecue chicken" and think of seriously sauced-up pieces that are slick and slippery and sweet. I like that kind of chicken just fine and have my own recipe for it, which I call "Wishbone Chicken" (page 36). However, in the traditional barbecue world, "barbecue chicken" is dry-rubbed, without sauce. This is my personal favorite way to prepare barbecue chicken. If you like, you can serve it with some sauce on the side. Sometimes, if we're not doing a Lowcountry Boil, I make this at our cooking school's Friday night dinner. It's simple to make and a great way to test out a new smoker and get your feet wet. I like to use eight-piece cut-up chickens instead of halves or quarters; this way you get more pieces with options for white and dark meat, and it's better for those who want only one piece. Notice this recipe calls for just chicken and rub—that's it.

Serves 4

1 small whole chicken, cut into 8 pieces
   (2 legs, 2 thighs, 2 wings, 2 breasts)

1 recipe Basic Chicken Rub (page 20)

Heat a smoker to 250°F.

Wash the chicken pieces thoroughly and pat them dry with paper towels. Apply the chicken rub all over the exposed areas of the chicken pieces. Place the seasoned chicken pieces in a deep aluminum baking pan, and place the pan in the smoker. Cook for 1½ hours.

Remove the wings, wrap them in aluminum foil, and keep them warm in an oven on the lowest setting. Return the rest of the chicken to the smoker and cook for an additional 1½ hours, or until the internal temperature of the white meat reaches 165°F and the dark meat reaches 180°F.

Remove the pan from the smoker. Allow the chicken to rest, uncovered, for 15 minutes. Then serve immediately.

Chicken Wings—Two Ways

To me, chicken wings are a delicacy. That's not because they're rare—believe me when I tell you that I eat them often—but because they're probably my favorite part of the yard bird. Wings are unique because you get two experiences in one: a drumette and what I call the "flat." That's two handles on one piece of meat for you to hold on to and enjoy. Wings also take very little time to prepare and cook. All you have to know is that before you cook them you have to cut off the tip, which is attached to the outer flat part of the joint. Using kitchen shears is an easy way to just lop it off—or use a sharp knife—and if you don't feel like throwing them away, put the tips in your freezer for the next time someone's making stock or soup.

Buffalo Wings

Makes 1 dozen

1½ tablespoons Chicken Sauce and
  Glaze (page 23)
1½ tablespoons hot sauce

2 teaspoons unsalted butter, melted
6 chicken wings
Vegetable oil, for deep-frying

In a large stainless steel bowl, combine the chicken sauce, hot sauce, and melted butter. Set aside.

Using a very sharp knife, cut each wing in half to separate the flat from the drumette. Wash the pieces well and pat them dry.

Heat a heavy, deep skillet, preferably cast-iron, over high heat. Pour enough oil into the hot skillet to come halfway up the sides. Heat the oil until it is hot and shimmering but not smoking (if using an electric skillet, heat it to 350°F).

Using tongs, carefully place the chicken wings in the hot oil. Fry the wings, turning them over halfway through, until golden brown, about 10 minutes.

Transfer the wings to paper towels to drain. Then quickly place them in the bowl of sauce and toss until they are coated evenly. Get your favorite condiment (mine is ranch dressing) and a good cold beer (mine is Stella), and enjoy immediately.

Barbecue Wings

Makes 1 dozen

6 chicken wings

2 cups Jack's Old South Huney Muney Cluck Rub, or 1 recipe Basic Chicken Rub (page 20)

1 recipe Chicken Sauce and Glaze (page 23)

Heat a smoker to 250°F.

Using a very sharp knife, cut each wing in half to separate the flat from the drumette.

Wash the pieces well and pat them dry. Apply the rub liberally to each piece. Place the chicken pieces in an aluminum baking pan and place the pan in the smoker. Cook, uncovered, for 2 hours.

Remove the pan from the smoker, brush the chicken sauce over the wings, and return the pan to the smoker. Cook for 15 minutes. Remove. Eat the hell out of 'em.

Wishbone Chicken

Nowadays chicken is cut into eight pieces: two legs, two thighs, two breasts, and two wings. Traditionally, though, when I was growing up, butchers used an eleven-piece cut: two legs, two thighs, two breasts, two wings, the neck, the back, and the wishbone. I created this recipe with the old-style cuts in mind because I like the way it gives you more pieces to enjoy and because it's an homage to an old-fashioned way of doing things. It's a recipe that relies on the flavors of smoke, of course, mingled with brown sugar, which caramelizes the skin. It's a wonderful take on classic saucy-style so-called barbecue chicken.

The easiest way to do this is to ask your butcher to cut up a whole chicken into eleven pieces. Then you're done. However, if you'd like to try it yourself, I've included instructions opposite.

Serves 4

2 cups chicken broth
1 cup (packed) dark brown sugar
1 small chicken (about 3 pounds), cut
    into 11 pieces
2 cups Jack's Old South Huney Muney
    Cluck Rub, or 1 recipe Basic Chicken
    Rub (page 20)

1½ cups (3 sticks) unsalted butter, at
    room temperature
1 recipe Chicken Sauce and Glaze
    (page 23)

In a large shallow dish, combine the chicken broth and brown sugar; stir well to dissolve the sugar. Marinate the chicken in this mixture, covered, in the refrigerator overnight.

When you are ready to cook the chicken, heat a smoker to 250°F.

Take the chicken out of the marinade and apply the rub liberally to all the pieces, being sure to season both sides of the wishbone. Place the pieces, skin side up, in a deep aluminum baking pan. Rub the chicken with some of the butter, and place the remaining butter in the pan. Place the pan in the smoker and cook for 30 minutes.

Remove the pan from the smoker, flip the chicken pieces so they are skin side down, and return the pan to the smoker. Cook for 1 hour or until the internal temperature of the chicken reaches 155°F.

Remove the pan from the smoker and sprinkle a little more rub over the chicken. Return it to the smoker and cook for 15 minutes.

Remove the pan from the smoker and brush the chicken sauce over the pieces. Return it to the smoker for another 15 minutes to let the sauce soak into the chicken.

Remove the pan from the smoker and let the chicken rest, uncovered, for 15 minutes. Then serve immediately. Don't forget to make a wish.

How to Cut Up a Chicken

Remove the giblets and neck from the chicken and either set them aside for stock or discard them. Rinse the chicken inside and out, and pat it dry thoroughly.

Orient the chicken so that its breast is facing up. Scrape at the shoulder to expose the wishbone. Once it is exposed, cut through the cartilage to loosen the prongs of the wishbone. Use your fingers to loosen the wishbone from the breast meat. Feel your way to the top, where it connects to the breastbone; then grab the top of the wishbone, give it a twist, and pull so it detaches. Remove the wishbone.

Pull a leg away from the body, and with a sharp knife, cut through the connecting skin and tissue to find the leg bone. Once the bone is reached, use the tip of your knife to find the joint where the thigh meets the body. Pressing the knife through the joint, cut through the cartilage and separate the leg from the body. Use your fingers to feel where the thigh bone meets the drumstick and cut through that joint with your knife. Once you've separated the drumstick from the thigh, look to see where you started your cut. On the other leg, look at the same region. You'll notice a line of fat. Cutting straight down through this line will yield a clean separation of drumstick and thigh. Next, separate the wing from the body. Repeat the leg and wing steps for the other side.

Rotate the carcass so it is breast side down. Using kitchen shears, cut through the ribs down both sides of the backbone. (If you don't have kitchen shears, you can stand the bird up and cut down with your knife to remove the backbone.) Split the breast by cutting through it, straight down the middle. Separate into two breasts.

Bacon-Wrapped Coca-Cola Chicken Breasts

Coca-Cola was born in Atlanta in 1886, when pharmacist Dr. John Stith Pemberton took his new creation to Jacobs' Pharmacy—where minutes after it was first sampled, it became a sensation. I love the stuff, in no small part because it's a fantastic global brand from Georgia . . . just like me. What a lot of people outside of the South don't realize is that Coke can be more than a "delicious and refreshing" drink; it's a great ingredient to use in a marinade because it's sweet and because the carbonation can be useful in tenderizing meat. It needs some balance, though, which is what the bacon does here: it adds a salty flavor and a crisp texture to the chicken. This dish is great for afternoon barbecues when you're chilling by the pool. Serve it with your favorite potato salad (see page 116).

Serves 2 to 4

4 small boneless, skinless chicken breasts (preferably from small chickens, about 1 pound total)
1 12-ounce can Coca-Cola
1 medium white onion, diced
2 cloves garlic, crushed
2 cups Jack's Old South Huney Muney Cluck Rub, or 1 recipe Basic Chicken Rub (page 20)
8 thin slices smoked bacon

Place the chicken breasts in a shallow dish, and add the Coca-Cola, onion, and garlic. Cover, and refrigerate overnight.

When you are ready to cook the chicken, preheat a smoker to 325°F.

Remove the chicken from the marinade and apply the rub liberally. Wrap each breast in 2 slices of the bacon, securing the slices with toothpicks. Place the breasts in an aluminum baking pan. Place the pan in the smoker and cook the breasts for 1 hour, or until their internal temperature reaches 165°F.

Remove the pan from the smoker and let the breasts rest, uncovered, in the pan for 15 minutes. Then slice the breasts and garnish them with any bacon that fell aside. My motto with this dish: Have a Coke and a breast, then smile.

Whole Chicken

Cooking a whole chicken in the smoker is probably the easiest thing you can master. I say that a whole hog (see page 53) isn't for beginners, but a whole chicken sure is.

Whenever you cook anything in a smoker, you risk drying it out. My chickens are never dry because the pan of apple juice underneath keeps the meat tender and circulates moisture and sweetness throughout the smoker. So the chicken is smoky in flavor and melt-in-your-mouth in texture. If you are a real "skin person," meaning the skin is your favorite part of the bird, you should know that the skin on this chicken becomes soft enough to bite through and is delicious (that said, if you prefer crunchy skin, see my fried chicken recipe on page 45).

If you like to make pulled chicken sandwiches, this is the recipe you need to start with. Simply cook this chicken and then, wearing food-handling gloves, pull the chicken meat from the bones and place it on a platter. Let your guests assemble their own sandwiches with buns and your favorite garnishes, such as Basic Hickory Sauce (page 22), Mama's Slaw (page 119), and pickles.

Serves 4 (or 8 for pulled chicken sandwiches)

1 small chicken (about 3 pounds), giblets removed
4 cups chicken broth
1 2-ounce packet dry onion soup mix

2 cups Jack's Old South Huney Muney Cluck Rub, or 1 recipe Basic Chicken Rub (page 20)
2 cups apple juice

Rinse the chicken inside and out, and pat it dry thoroughly. Place the chicken in a deep pan, add the broth and soup mix, and marinate, covered, in the refrigerator overnight.

When you are ready to cook the chicken, preheat a smoker to 250°F.

Remove the pan from the refrigerator and discard the marinade. Apply the rub liberally to the chicken. Place the chicken, breast side up, on a meat rack with the handles down so the bird will be raised above the surface of the pans. Set the rack inside a deep aluminum pan. Pour the apple juice into the pan underneath the meat rack. Place the pan in the smoker and cook for 3 hours or until the breast meat reaches 165°F. Remove the chicken from the smoker and allow it to rest on the rack in its pan for 15 minutes. To serve, carve the chicken into individual pieces.

Apple and Bacon—Stuffed Chicken Breasts

Serves 4

1 yellow apple, such as Golden
    Delicious, peeled, cored, and chopped
6 slices bacon, fried and crumbled
4 large boneless, skinless chicken breasts
    (at least 12 ounces each)

2 cups Jack's Old South Huney Muney
    Cluck Rub, or 1 recipe Basic Chicken
    Rub (page 20)
1 cup apple juice

Heat a smoker to 300°F.

In a small bowl, combine the chopped apple and bacon.

Using a sharp paring knife, cut a pocket about 3 inches deep in the thickest side of each chicken breast. Spoon the apple mixture into the pockets and secure the openings with toothpicks.

Apply the rub to the outside of the chicken breasts. Put the breasts in a large aluminum baking pan, and place the pan in the smoker. Cook, spritzing the chicken with apple juice every 15 minutes, for 1 hour or until the internal temperature of each breast reaches 165°F.

Remove the pan from the smoker and allow the chicken to rest, loosely covered, for 10 minutes. Serve.

Smoked Turkey

We go to my wife's family's Thanksgiving dinner every year and it's one of my rare days off from cooking, but the truth is that I love to smoke turkey and I don't believe in waiting for Thanksgiving to enjoy it. It's an excellent way to feed a crowd at any celebration. And I believe dark meat and white meat are equally delicious, so I make sure I get some of both. Encourage your guests to do the same. And if you've never considered it before, you might try pulling the meat off the bird the same way you would when making pulled chicken (see page 40) to have pulled turkey sandwiches. They're good, too.

Serves 10 to 12

1 12- to 15-pound turkey, neck and
   giblets removed
8 cups chicken broth
3 medium white onions, diced
4 cloves garlic, crushed

1 cup (packed) dark brown sugar
2 cups Jack's Old South Huney Muney
   Cluck Rub, or 1 recipe Basic Chicken
   Rub (page 20)

Rinse the turkey inside and out, and pat it dry thoroughly. Place the turkey in a large roasting bag, and add the chicken broth, onions, garlic, and brown sugar. Tie the bag to seal it and place it in a large roasting pan. Allow the turkey to marinate this way in the refrigerator overnight.

When you are ready to cook the turkey, heat a smoker to 250°F.

Remove the turkey from the bag, and discard the marinade. Apply the rub all over the bird. Put the turkey on a rack in a large, deep aluminum pan, place the pan in the smoker, and cook for 5 hours or until the breast meat reaches an internal temperature of 165°F.

Remove the pan from the smoker. Allow the turkey to rest, loosely covered with foil, for 30 minutes. Then carve the turkey, and serve immediately.

Myron's Signature Buttermilk Fried Chicken

Fried chicken is a Southern staple, and to be a good Southern cook you better know how to make it. I do. I like to use small fresh chickens for frying because the flavor of the meat is better. And speaking of flavor, I like to fry my chicken in pure pork lard, which gives it a richness and down-home essence that vegetable oil just can't replicate. You can buy good high-quality lard—and I'm not talking about the soapy-looking white blocks sold in some supermarkets—from any reputable butcher. What makes my fried chicken special is the mixture of spices I use—note that both chili powder and sugar are involved—and the tangy richness that buttermilk lends.

Serves 4

2 cups all-purpose flour

1 tablespoon salt

2 tablespoons finely ground black pepper

1 teaspoon garlic powder

1 teaspoon onion powder

1 teaspoon chili powder

1 teaspoon sugar

1 teaspoon smoked sweet paprika

2 eggs

4 cups buttermilk

1 small chicken (about 3 pounds), cut into 8 pieces (2 legs, 2 thighs, 2 breasts, 2 wings)

1 to 1½ cups pork lard, vegetable oil, or peanut oil

In a large bowl, combine all the dry ingredients. Mix together with a fork until thoroughly combined. Set aside.

In another large bowl, beat the eggs into the buttermilk. Coat the chicken pieces in the egg-and-buttermilk mixture, and then dredge them in the seasoned flour. Repeat, coating the chicken again with the egg-and-buttermilk mixture and then dredging them again in the seasoned flour mixture, to create a double layer of batter. Set the pieces on a clean platter.

Pour the lard or oil to a depth of 1 inch in a large cast-iron skillet, and heat it over medium heat until the temperature reaches 325°F on a deep-frying thermometer. Add the chicken pieces, in batches, and cook for about 20 minutes, turning them over halfway through cooking. The wings will be done after 10 minutes. Drain the chicken thoroughly on paper towels, and serve immediately.

4

I am fond of pigs. Dogs look up to us.
Cats look down on us. Pigs treat us as equals.
—Sir Winston Churchill

I'M NOT BRAGGING when I say that pork has been a stellar category for me at barbecue competitions. I mean it only makes sense since it's the meat I grew up cooking, and so everything that has to do with it is second nature for me. It's also a damn near perfect match in terms of the way I like to cook, because pork's generally mild flavor pairs perfectly with the sweetness of most fruits and by now y'all know that I prefer to cook with fruit woods (see page 8). If I wasn't good at cooking hogs, I'd have to learn it, because it's damn near impossible to create grand championship–winning barbecue without knowing your way around a hog. I'm not saying you have to have worked in an abattoir; what I'm saying is that you can't master barbecue and skip over hog cooking. It's an essential skill of the trade. It's also very rewarding, of course, because after you're done cooking a hog or even just its shoulder, you get to eat something that's as close to heaven as you're ever likely to put in your mouth.

Cooking hogs makes me think about growing up, and that makes me think about my dad. My dad died so unexpectedly: One minute he was Jack Mixon, larger than life, kicking ass and talking names as usual, talking about the last big fish he caught (my dad loved to fish). The next minute, he had a stroke. It shook up my life like you wouldn't believe. I wasn't counting on not having him around to advise me, as he had always done.

So I found myself in a predicament: I lost my dad, I'd been recently divorced, and I had to figure out how to make the payments on my truck. (People ask me about what motivates me to win contests. It's easy: You ever not know where your next truck payment was going to come from? That's some powerful motivation.) I had the legacy of my parents' hickory barbecue sauce. I had a town that knew my name meant "barbecue." So I looked around at what was going on in the world of competitive barbecue cooking. With a few notable exceptions—like Mike Mills and his Apple City Barbecue Team from Murphysboro, Illinois, who were the top dogs in those days—a lot of folks on the circuit were hobbyists who were there for the fun and camaraderie. I understood that, but I also understood that there was serious money to be made, and I'd be damned if I wasn't going to try to get at it.

Now, cooking a hog wasn't a problem for me—I'd seen my daddy do it countless times in his homemade pits, whose near-constant stoking was my boyhood job. What I had to learn, though, was what the judges were looking for and how I could create it. At Memphis in May events, whole hog is the key category. You are visited in person by a judge who actually comes to your cooking camp, sits down, and eats while you answer questions about how you prepared your meat. The judge is considering the taste and tenderness of your hog as well as its appearance. The appearance score is about the eye appeal of the meat on the grill, and garnish can be used to enhance this. That right there was new to me.

The deal is that when an MIM judge comes to your cook site, the rules state that you must present your hog on the smoker. At my first contest, which I entered in June 1996, I had a very dim idea of how to deal with the presentation part of things—I was a lone wolf at that contest, and I had nobody to advise me on the best way to handle my show. Common sense told me that I needed garnishes that could withstand some heat without withering and shriveling up, and that they needed to be things that would look natural next to a gigantic cooked pig. I thought: I've got to use hardy fruits and vegetables that can withstand the heat of the smoker. I figured on kale as the best choice for a base because it doesn't dry out like lettuce. Then I placed a pineapple, some oranges, and some lemons around the hog in an attractive pattern. I did the best I could, and when I stood back to take a look at the results I thought I'd done a damn good job. And when the results

were announced, sure enough I came in first place on whole hog. "This ain't nothing," I said to myself, thinking as a first-timer that I'd pulled one over on everybody in the contest. Taking that first in whole hog was so easy, it seemed like spitting off a train.

Well, I was thirty-four years old then and I didn't know any better. I can tell you now that what happened to me was beginner's luck. I can also tell you that I haven't changed a whole lot about the way I cook and present hogs since, either. My main idea, then and now and probably always, is that hog should taste full-flavored, tangy, rich (there's an

awful lot of fat on a pig, after all), and complex—in other words, it should taste like meat, because a barbecue contest is a meat contest. So the pork shouldn't taste like maple syrup or cherries or grape jelly, even if you use those ingredients in your marinade or glaze. What should come through is the deliciously mild flavor of pork kissed with smoke.

My hogs taste the same way every time I cook them. People don't believe me when I say that, but trust me when I tell you that it's true. Why? First of all there's consistency: I've been cooking hogs for a long time, and I can predictably tell you how one's going to turn

out provided that I take care to follow all my trusted steps. Second, I've got a method I can depend on. For instance, I never turn my hogs once they're in the smoker. I know that a lot of people like to, and that a lot of barbecue cookbooks are full of information about how to organize the turning of the beast and things like that. Well, I cook my hogs on their backs without ever turning them because I want to keep all the flavors I've added to them contained in one place. In my way of doing things, the skin of the hog acts like a bowl to hold the flavors and juices in, and turning it would spoil the effect. It works like a charm, so why would you make hog cooking any harder than it needs to be?

The other thing I had to figure out when it comes to pork is how to "build my box." What this means is that in both MIM and KCBS competitions, we have to turn in a plain white Styrofoam box filled with meat. In addition to the judging process that places the judges right in front of you, they also do blind judging. We all spend a lot of time worrying over how to keep the meat nice and moist and tender in that box because the second you cut it up and it gets exposed to air, it starts drying out. I don't mind telling you that I'm known for making some of the most attractive boxes on the circuit. I'm not going to lie to you, either: I spend a lot of time thinking about how to set up my hog boxes. I have a whole philosophy about it: You want the box to look like you just reached into the pig and set the meat out. You want it to look fresh and appealing. And that can be tricky, because if you follow all the requirements and include the right kinds of meat, you're dealing with a two-pound box of food by the time you're finished. What does this have to do with you? Well, I reckon that when you feed your own crowd, you want your food to look pretty good, too.

It's a great event to cook a whole hog: you can feed your entire neighborhood, your church congregation, your local political caucus, or whoever it is you like to impress. But you don't have to make it hard for yourself if you don't feel like it. You can make a shoulder instead and have the best barbecue sandwiches you ever tasted. You can make kick-ass pork chops. You can use my hog-cooking recipes as tools, learn how to apply my formulas, and then you can do your own damn delicious thing.

Whole Hog

A whole hog can weigh anywhere from 75 to 180 pounds. I like to cook the big ones the best, because they've got the most meat on them and can serve a huge crowd. Now, some 'cue cookers may tell you that smaller is better because it's easier to handle, but I don't truck with that. The quality of the meat on a smaller hog is no different than a bigger one, and if you're going to go to all the trouble to smoke a whole hog, then you might as well get as much as you can for your efforts. For more than eight years now, I've been buying my hogs from Elmer Yoder at his business, Yoder's Butcher Block. He is located in a rural Mennonite community about fourteen miles from my home in Unadilla, Georgia. I get my hogs from Yoder's not just because he's close to where I live but also because the quality of Yoder's meat is very high. His heritage demands it. I know I can count on Yoder to supply me hormone- and drug-free meats that are as naturally raised as possible. Raising animals this way is a skill that has been overshadowed by the large meat processors, but Yoder has found his niche here, processing deer and hogs and everything in between, and he has dedicated customers. The quality of his pork is top-tier. End of day, he helps me be a champion.

Now, in other parts of the country it is hard to find whole hogs. My best suggestion is to order one from a good, reputable butcher. A few things to know when ordering a hog: First, determine what size will fit in your smoker. Measure the inside length of your cooking chamber. It needs to be at least four feet to be able to cook a 50- to 80-pound hog, and five to six feet if you want to cook a bigger one (up to about 200 pounds). Tell the butcher that you want the hog to be "round," which means split and gutted but not butterflied (you'll do that yourself and then you can be sure to lay it out like you want it). Getting a hog this way saves a whole lot of time and energy. I like the head left on but the feet removed for presentation purposes, but that part is up to you.

If you want to cook a whole hog, this recipe will take you through every step. But if you really want to know how to cook whole hog like a professional, I suggest that you attend my barbecue class (or a good local barbecue class) to familiarize yourself with the process. Cooking a whole hog is not for the faint of heart, and it sure ain't for first-timers.

1 180-pound hog, gutted and split

3 recipes Hog Injection (page 21)

9 cups Jack's Old South Original Rub, or 3 recipes Basic Barbecue Rub (page 20)

3 recipes Hog Glaze (page 23)

2 boneless pork shoulders (Boston butt only) or 2 brisket flats (about 6 pounds each)

What you'll need:

Meat saw

1 heavy-duty injector

Brush (a kitchen basting brush could be used, but a larger unused paintbrush will save you time)

At least one helper (as you'll need someone to help you carry the whole hog)

On a long table covered with clean butcher paper or other sanitary covering, lay long strips of aluminum foil. Place the hog flat on its back on top of the foil. With a very sharp butcher knife, score (i.e., make shallow cuts in the meat) along each side of the spine of the hog, where the ribs connect. Then crack and pull down each side of the hog, starting from the spine. You want the hog to be lying semi-flat so that you can easily reach inside.

Following the instructions on page 76, remove the membrane (or "silver") from the backs of the ribs on each side. Trim away any excess fat on the hams, shoulders, and along the rib cage.

Using a meat saw, split and saw down between the ribs and down each side of the hog: You're going to cut the ribs on both sides three inches off the spine. This is basically making baby back ribs out of the full spares. Saw only the bone, trying not to pierce the skin on the bottom of the hog. (This makes it easier, after cooking, to serve ribs from the hog.)

Separate the picnic ham of the shoulder from the Boston butt. Again, trim both hams of any excess fat. When prepping the shoulder, there is a membrane that you can feel with a knife that separates the Boston butt end, which is next to the spine, from the picnic ham (or shank). Cut through the membrane, making sure not to cut through the skin. This lays the shoulder so it can crust over and have a good bark.

Load the hog injection into your injector. Out of habit, I always start by injecting the hams first and then I work my way to the head. I inject in seven locations all over the ham, making sure the ham is full to the point of popping. It doesn't matter where exactly you inject so long as it's all over the hog. A word of caution: Don't make more injection holes than necessary, because more holes means more places for the marinade to leak out. Move to the sides of the cavity where the bacon is. It will be covered by the ribs. Inject all along both sides. There are two tenderloins at the end of the spine near the hams. Inject them carefully and do not over-inject (or shoot too much fluid in); if the fluid begins leaking out, you'll know that you've done more than enough. Then move to the shortened ribs that have been cut and inject straight down between the ribs directly against the spine into the loin. Remember not to push the needle through the skin on the bottom of the hog's back. Now inject the shoulder, butt, and shank (picnic ham). Last, inject the cheek meat (or jowl) along the hog's jawbone.

Sprinkle the rub throughout the cavity and on the surface of any exposed meat. (Some people think you have to actually "rub" the rub into the meat, but I don't think that does anything to the taste.) Gather up the foil you've laid the hog on and use it to wrap the entire hog loosely.

Let the hog sit for 1 hour to soak up all the injection. During this time, light the smoker and bring it to 250°F.

Place the 2 shoulders or brisket flats in the smoker, and then carefully place the hog on top of the shoulders/brisket, so that the extra meat runs the length of the hog directly under the center. Close the smoker and let the hog smoke for about 20 hours, or until the internal temperature of the meatiest part of the shoulder is 205°F. (I often set my hog on the smoker at noon the day before I want to eat it; then I remove it at 8 a.m. the next morning.)

Unwrap the foil, and using a brush, apply the hog glaze throughout the inside of the cavity and on the hams. Rewrap the hog loosely in the foil. Leaving the hog on the smoker, let the temperature fall (no more wood is needed at this point). The glaze will caramelize and set while the hog begins to rest and cool down enough so that folks can start pulling the meat. (Unless you're a professional caterer or otherwise need to present the whole hog, the hog is left in the smoker while it is picked and pulled and, best of all, eaten.)

In true Southern tradition, a whole hog is never "carved" per se. Wearing clean heavy-duty gloves and using either large tongs or your hands, gently pull the meat out of the hog in chunks and pile it onto large trays or straight onto plates.

A Word on Cooking Hog Loins

Now, the most difficult part of cooking the whole hog properly is the loin, which tends to cook faster than the tougher, bigger, and denser hams and shoulders. I solve this problem by placing a cheaper cut of meat, such as a boneless butt or brisket flat, underneath the hog down the length of the backbone. This will add another barrier between the loin and the heat from the smoker, helping to keep it moist and not overcooked. That's why this recipe (see page 53) calls for adding two shoulders or brisket flats: it will keep your loin from over-cooking. And the type of meat you choose won't matter, as it won't be fit for a buzzard when you're through cooking the hog.

Pork Shoulder

Pork shoulder is what they call the top of the front leg of the hog; it's not exactly a shoulder, but if you think about it, it kind of is. It is comprised of two parts: The lower (or "arm") portion of the shoulder is most commonly called the "picnic" or "picnic ham." True ham comes only from the hind legs; the picnic of the shoulder, though, is often smoked like ham, and some historians speculate that it got its nickname because it's inexpensive and thus a good cut for casual dining, not for a formal affair when a "real" ham is traditionally served, like at Easter, Thanksgiving, or Christmas. The upper part of the shoulder, often called the "Boston butt," also known as a "Boston blade roast," comes from the area near the loin and contains the shoulder blade bone. It is an inexpensive cut that's packed with muscle, and so without proper tenderizing and cooking it can be unmanageably tough. However, it is well marbled and full of flavorful fat, and thus is ideal for smoking over low temperature; it is the classic meat used for all "pulled pork" in barbecue throughout the South.

At Memphis in May contests, which are the first ones I learned to cook for, the whole pork shoulder is always used. At KCBS contests, you can use either a whole shoulder or the Boston butt by itself. I'm used to cooking the whole thing, so that's what I usually do. History and contest rules aside, here's the best way in the world to cook a pork shoulder.

Serves 30 to 40

1 18- to 20-pound pork shoulder, including the Boston butt and picnic ham in one cut (this may have to be ordered from a butcher; in many supermarkets the cuts are preseparated)

1 recipe Hog Injection (page 21)
3 cups Jack's Old South Original Rub, or 1 recipe Basic Barbecue Rub (page 20)
1 cup apple juice
1 recipe Hog Glaze (page 23)

Trim away any bone slivers from the exposed meat. Remove any visible excess fat. Square up the long sides of the shoulder to make it neat and uniform.

Place the pork shoulder in a large aluminum pan. (There's no skin to hold the liquid in, as there is on a whole hog, so the pan is necessary to catch the excess liquid.) Inject the shoulder with

2 to 3 quarts of the hog injection, all over the shoulder in about 1-inch squares. Let the injected shoulder sit, loosely covered, in the refrigerator for 2 hours.

Turn the shoulder upside-down in the pan, so that any excess injection that might remain infuses the meat. Let it sit upside-down for 15 to 20 minutes.

In the meantime, heat a smoker to 250°F.

Take the shoulder out of the pan and sprinkle the rub all over it, making sure to get the area by the shank. Place the shoulder, in its aluminum pan, in the smoker and cook for 3 hours.

Remove the shoulder from the smoker. Pour the apple juice into a clean aluminum pan, and transfer the shoulder to the pan. Cover the pan with aluminum foil and place it in the smoker. Cook for 6 hours or until the internal temperature reaches 205°F.

Remove the pan from the smoker. Discard the foil. Brush the hog glaze all over both sides of the shoulder. Return the shoulder to the pan, put the pan back in the smoker, and cook for 1 more hour while adding no more heat to the smoker and allowing the internal temperature of the smoker to drop. The shoulder will effectively rest in the smoker this way.

Remove the pan from the smoker, and serve. Where I'm from, a pork shoulder is not sliced—it's pulled apart in chunks. There are a couple of different ways to do it, with knives and tongs and such, but the very best—and easiest—is with your hands. Wearing heavy-duty gloves, simply pull the meat apart gently and let your guests have at it. You can put it in a sandwich just like this, or you can chop it up after you've pulled it, if you like.

Why Boston?

I used to wonder why this part of the shoulder was called "Boston" anything, since it's so associated with Southern barbecue. The folks from the National Pork Board say it plain: "In pre-revolutionary New England and into the Revolutionary War, some pork cuts (not those highly valued, or 'high on the hog,' like loin and ham) were packed into casks or barrels (also known as 'butts') for storage and shipment." So, the way the hog shoulder was cut in the Boston area became known in other regions as "Boston butt."

Half and Half

Here's a tip from my competitive barbecue cooking that you can use in your backyard. I make a little solution I call "half and half." It's equal parts vinegar sauce and water, and I heat it up until it's hot but not boiling. Then I dip pieces of shoulder in it before I put them in the judging box. Why do I do this? Because it keeps the meat from drying out and getting cold. You always want your meat to stay moist and warm. You can do this at home, too. Before you serve any meat like brisket or pork shoulder, toss it with a little half and half and then put it on a platter. Better yet, apply the solution to the back side of slices of brisket and pork before you place them on a platter. This technique will keep your meat from drying out.

Cracklin' Skins

When you cook a whole hog, one thing you should never do is throw out the skin. It's the key ingredient for one of the tastiest by-products in the world. If you're not cooking a whole hog, I'm not going to fool you by saying it's easy to pick up some pig skin, but you might be able to get some from your local butcher or from someone who is cooking a whole hog, a ham, or a pork shoulder and is willing to part with it.

Serves 6 to 8

Hog skin from a whole hog, ham, or shoulder
Kosher salt

Preheat the oven to 300°F.

Scrape any fat and meat off the skin, leaving only the skin. Using kitchen shears, cut the skin into cracker-size pieces. Place the skin pieces on top of a cooling rack in a large sheet pan, and sprinkle them with kosher salt. Cook in the oven until the fat is rendered in the bottom of the sheet pan and the skin is golden brown and crispy, usually about 3½ hours.

Remove the pan from the oven and place the skins on paper towels to drain and cool.

Dust the cracklings with your favorite rub or dip them into your favorite barbecue sauce.

Smoked Jack Bologna

No, this dish was not inspired by my father, Jack. It gets its name from the pepper jack cheese that you use to stuff the bologna. Many Memphis in May competition teams cook this dish at the annual World Championship and snack on it during the weeklong celebration.

Serves 10 to 12

1 6½-pound good-quality bologna
1 pound pepper jack cheese, cut into
  ½-inch cubes
3 cups Jack's Old South Hickory Sauce,
  or 1 recipe Basic Hickory Sauce
  (page 22)

1 large loaf crusty sourdough bread,
  sliced
Prepared mustard, to taste
Louisiana hot sauce, to taste
1 Vidalia or other sweet onion, sliced

Heat a smoker to 250°F.

Remove the bulb end of a turkey baster. Use the wide end of the baster to core through the middle of the log of bologna and remove a long tube of the meat; reserve two 2-inch-long pieces. Fill the open core with the pepper jack cubes, and then plug the ends with the reserved pieces of bologna. Put the bologna in a large aluminum pan, place it in the smoker, and cook for 1½ hours.

Remove the pan from the smoker, and glaze the bologna with the hickory sauce. Return it to the smoker and cook for 15 minutes or until the sauce is thoroughly caramelized.

Remove the pan from the smoker. Let the bologna rest in the pan, loosely covered, for 10 minutes.

Slice the bologna into ¾-inch-thick slices. Place each slice on a piece of sourdough bread. Slather the meat with mustard, add a few drips of hot sauce, and top with slices of sweet onion. Cover with another slice of bread and serve as a sandwich.

Sausage—Two Ways

The world of sausages is large and consists of any kind of meat mixture (or fish, or even vegetable if you want to get loose about it) that is stuffed into a casing, and they've existed as a way to preserve food—let's be honest, it started with meat—since antiquity. Sausages encompass everything from American hot dogs to French saucisson, to German bratwurst, to Italian salami, to Portuguese chorizo, to an entire system of traditional British sausages. In southern Georgia, the sausage of choice is smoked sausage. I'm talking about Polish kielbasa-style sausage that's made with coarsely ground pork, seasoned heavily with sage, garlic, and black pepper, and then is smoked to perfection so that it comes in big, fat, brown-red rings. It's salty and lusty and really good with a cold pilsner. It's also very, very versatile. Here are my two favorite ways of enjoying smoked sausage.

Grilled Sausage

Serves 4

1 pound smoked sausage, sliced crosswise into quarters and then in half lengthwise

4 fresh hoagie rolls

4 tablespoons hot pickle relish

4 teaspoons prepared mustard, preferably spicy brown

Build a charcoal fire or preheat a gas grill.

Place the sausages on the cooking grate over direct medium heat. Cook, turning them occasionally to mark all sides, until the skin starts to split, 6 to 8 minutes.

Slide the sausages onto the buns and top with the hot relish and mustard.

Redneck Sausage Hors d'Oeuvres

Serves 4

1 pound smoked sausage, cut into
  rounds about ½ inch thick
3 cups Jack's Old South Original Rub,
  or 1 recipe Basic Barbecue Rub
  (page 20)

3 cups Jack's Old South Hickory Sauce,
  or 1 recipe Basic Hickory Sauce
  (page 22)

Heat a smoker to 300°F.

Place the sausage slices in a single layer on an aluminum baking pan, and sprinkle them liberally with the rub. Put the pan in the smoker and let the sausages smoke for 45 minutes. Check occasionally to make sure they're not sticking to the pan.

Remove the pan from the smoker, and toss the sausages with the hickory sauce. Place toothpicks in the slices and arrange on a platter. And there you have it: redneck hors d'oeuvres.

Pork Burgers

I love burgers made from freshly ground meat. If you have access to your own meat grinder, grind up a fresh boneless Boston butt with the onions. If you don't, don't worry about it. These burgers aren't quite as over the top as my Whistler Burger (page 98), but they're flavorful as hell and a really nice change if you feel like eating something other than beef.

Serves 8

2 pounds ground pork
3 yellow onions, finely diced
1 teaspoon salt
½ cup coarsely ground black pepper
1 cup Jack's Old South Hickory Sauce
   or Basic Hickory Sauce (page 22)

8 onion or cheese rolls, split
Prepared brown mustard (optional)
Sliced dill pickles (optional)

Heat a smoker to 350°F.

In a large bowl, combine all the ingredients. Form the mixture into eight 4-ounce patties. Place the patties in a large aluminum pan, and set the pan in the smoker. Cook for about 7 minutes.

Remove the pan from the smoker and flip the burgers. Return the pan to the smoker and cook for 8 more minutes.

Serve the burgers on onion or cheese rolls, topped with brown mustard and dill pickles, if you like.

Pork Loin

Pork roast is such a crowd-pleaser, so next time you make one, why not try it on the smoker? It's incredibly easy and it doesn't take much time. It also doesn't make your kitchen hot and crowded, either. It's always better, to me, to get the meat cooking outside—it frees up a lot of space for preparing the rest of the meal.

Serves 6

> 1 3½- to 4-pound boneless pork loin
> 1 recipe Hog Injection (page 21)
> 3 cups Jack's Old South Original Rub,
>   or 1 recipe Basic Barbecue Rub
>   (page 20)
> 1 recipe Tangy Sweet Sauce (page 23)

Place the pork roast in a medium aluminum pan. Inject the loin with hog injection and let it rest, covered, in the refrigerator for 4 hours.

When you are ready to cook the pork, heat a smoker to 350°F.

Remove the pan from the refrigerator, and coat the pork all over with the rub. Place it back in the pan, put the pan in the smoker, and cook for 1½ hours or until its internal temperature reaches 155°F.

Remove the pan from the smoker and brush the tangy sweet sauce all over the pork. Return it to the smoker and cook for 15 minutes.

Remove the pan from the smoker and let the loin rest, loosely covered, for 30 minutes. Then slice it into ½-inch-thick slices and serve.

Stuffed Pork Tenderloin

Sometimes when you're barbecuing, you want to get a little fancy—maybe to impress the neighbors or something like that. Hell, I've been there, believe me. And I can tell you from experience that stuffed tenderloin will get you that "wow" factor.

Serves 4

1 large pork tenderloin (about 1½ pounds)
1 pound smoked sausage (a large link)
3 cups Jack's Old South Original Rub, or 1 recipe Basic Barbecue Rub (page 20)

3½ cups Jack's Old South Vinegar Sauce, or 1 recipe Basic Vinegar Sauce (page 22)
2 cups apple jelly

Heat a smoker to 300°F.

Trim any excess fat and membrane from the pork tenderloin. Using a sharp knife with a very long, straight blade, insert the knife through the center of the tenderloin. Take care not to cut out to the sides—just insert the knife blade into the center and then remove it. Push a turkey baster through the cut, enlarging the opening; remove the baster.

Trim your smoked sausage link to the exact length of the tenderloin. Stuff it into the opening. Apply the rub thoroughly, coating the outside of the tenderloin. Place the tenderloin in a medium-size aluminum pan, and place the pan in the smoker. Cook for about 1 hour or until the internal temperature of the meat reaches 150°F.

While the meat is cooking, prepare the sauce: In a medium saucepan over medium heat, combine the vinegar sauce and the apple jelly. Stir thoroughly to combine. Make sure the sauce thins out as it heats, about 5 minutes. Then lower the heat and keep it warm until you're ready to use it.

During the last 15 minutes of cooking time, apply half of the sauce to the meat and put the meat back in the smoker. Reserve the remaining sauce.

Remove the pan from the smoker. Allow the meat to sit, loosely covered, for 10 minutes. Then cut it into slices about ¼ to ½ inch thick, and serve with the remaining sauce.

Ribs and Chops

If Fred Flintstone knew that the large order of ribs would tip his car over, why did he order them at the end of every show?
—Steven Wright

HAVE YOU READ the Bible? Let's just say that some select sections of it were forced on me by my mama, who is a true believer and threatens to this day to wash my mouth out with soap whenever I use the Lord's name in vain. That aside, one thing that stuck with me was the lesson of Adam and Eve in the Garden of Eden. I often ask people: "Do you know how I know that Adam wasn't from the South? Because no true Southerner would ever give up a rib."

For some people, ribs are the beginning, middle, and end of the barbecue conversation. Even more than a whole hog, which is sacred to true barbecue believers, ribs are the iconic image that comes to mind for most people when they hear the word "barbecue." The funny thing is that it doesn't even matter which kind of ribs people are talking about. They most likely mean pork ribs (though there are other and arguably equally tasty ribs, like barbecued beef ones). They could mean St. Louis ribs, also called spareribs, which are long and come from the bottom belly and shoulder portion of the hog. Or they could mean baby back ribs, which are the ribs that separate the loin section from the tenderloin; they are small and do not contain any of the backbone. There's a considerable difference between the two types of pork ribs and different people may have their preferences, but it seems like everyone who eats has a soft spot for ribs.

There are a lot of theories as to why. I believe it's because ribs, like most of the best comfort foods, have built-in "handles" and are just easy to hold and eat. Take corn dogs, hamburgers, pizza, chicken legs, and turkey legs. We gravitate to these foods because they're convenient and simple to grip, and also because they taste so damn good. It's an irresistible combination. What some people don't realize is that in competition, ribs are a linchpin to success. To understand that, you have to know a thing or two about how the competition circuit works.

In this country, two main organizations sanction official barbecue contests, and they establish the rules and regulations that govern the events. One is the Memphis in May Sanctioned Contest Network, which oversees the gigantic Memphis in May World Championship Barbecue Cooking Contest as well as many other competitions. The actual event called "Memphis in May" is a monthlong party with music and all sorts of festivities, but what I'm interested in, of course, is the barbecue contest. It has been held since 1977. The other sanctioning body is the Kansas City Barbecue Society (KCBS), which oversees the Jack Daniel's World Championship, and that contest has been held on the fourth Saturday in October since 1989. A main difference between the two is that MIM events are hog-only, while KCBS ones include beef and other meats. Another key difference: At MIM contests, judges come to your booth and you have to put on a show. I'm not kidding: You literally have to show the judges your cooker, tell them how you cooked the meat, and then feed them. The judges are looking to be entertained as much as they're looking to be well fed. Food is the most important component of any contest, but trust me when I tell you that the judges want the damn show. (You can read more about this in the Hog chapter.) At KCBS contests there's a blind judging of all the meat, and according to contest rules you have to arrange your meat artfully in a Styrofoam box, showing it to its best advantage, because appearance really counts. Both of these governing bodies of barbecue sponsor qualifying contests throughout the year, and the big ones have both open and invitational sections. "Open" just means that anyone can enter; "invitational" means you have to receive an invitation to compete, which you get when you have won a prior contest. What folks don't always realize is that the meat you bring to contests may not be marinated, injected, cured, rubbed, or otherwise treated or flavored in any way before the contest begins and it's officially inspected. So it's really impossible for you to have any tricks up your sleeve. You have to just cook

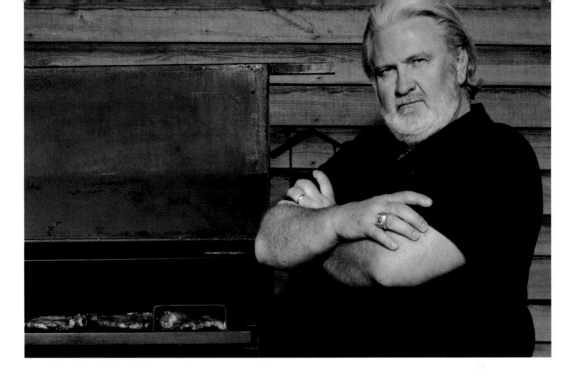

In order to be the man you have to beat the man ... and I'm the man.

the best way you can, which is pretty much all you can do in your own backyard, too.

I bring all of this up now because ribs are a category that transcends it all: ribs are equally important in both sanctions. I base what I cook on what the judges like, because I want to win. So that means if I'm doing a MIM contest, I cook baby backs. In a KCBS contest, I cook St. Louis. Either way, ribs have always been a good category for my team. In ribs, I've been MIM "team of the year" six times. A big part of my success is in

understanding what the judges want. And what the judges look for in a winning rib is a perfect combination of texture (soft without being mushy), flavor (smoky, but with a sweet glaze), and appearance (shiny like new pennies). In competition, ribs are prized for their heavily smoked flavor. This plays beautifully with the sweet sauce. You want ribs that are tender, with the perfect balance of sweetness and smoke.

Also, that glistening look is important, and with ribs you have to work to get the color right. I'll show you how to do it. That said, the hardest part of rib cooking is making them tender without overcooking them. I'll show you how to do that, too.

Mastering Pork Ribs

Types of Ribs

St. Louis ribs, or **spareribs,** are generally the least expensive cut of ribs; they are the long bones from the lower part of the hog's belly behind its shoulder. They are long, straight, and often fattier than baby backs.

Baby back ribs, or **loin back ribs,** come from the top of the hog's rib cage between the spine and the spareribs; they separate the loin from the tenderloin. They are shorter, curved, and often meatier than spareribs.

Country-style ribs are the blade end of a bone-in pork loin, close to the shoulder. They are big hunks of meat that contain no actual rib bones, so some folks who don't like to mess with bones prefer to cook them. They are full of meat but they turn mushy fast, so they need careful watching.

Kansas City–style ribs are spareribs that have the breastbone and skirt removed. Essentially they are spareribs that have been trimmed as much as they possibly can be so that what remains is merely a rectangle of meat and bone.

Rib Buying Guide

These tips apply to all varieties of ribs: Look for slabs with meat showing over the whole slab, with no bones or ribs that have been cut away down to the bone and no rib bone showing through the meat (these are called "shiners" and are especially prevalent in baby backs). With spareribs, there's usually some fat covering the first three ribs, which can easily be trimmed. Don't buy spareribs with lots of fat pockets or that are covered entirely in fat; these will be very hard to cook to tenderness and won't leave much to eat when they're done cooking. Fresh ribs that have never been frozen are better than the frozen ones, which risk freezer burn and may become mushy during the thawing process (and of course all meat should be defrosted before cooking).

Cooking Tips

Racks of St. Louis ribs usually weigh 3.8 pounds or less, and are generally referred to by professionals according to this weight, as in "3½ and down" or "3.8 and down."

The general rule for St. Louis ribs: Smoke at 275°F for 3 hours; rest in pan for 1 hour.

Racks of baby backs can weigh from ½ to 2¼ pounds each; they run about a dollar or so more per rack than spareribs, but you get loin and tenderloin meat on them and you don't have to trim any bone.

The general rule for baby back ribs: Smoke at 250°F for 2 hours; rest in the pan for 1 hour.

The general rule for handling any type of ribs: Always put them in the pan upside-down; this makes it much easier to roll them over when they're hot and it's time to glaze them.

Spritzing

One thing I picked up during my years competing is the technique of using a spray bottle to spritz my ribs with a special solution. Spritzing is an ingenious way to keep the outside (or "bark") of the rib moist during cooking, plus it adds another level of flavor to the ribs. People always look at me funny when I prepare my spritz and they see that I use imitation butter, which comes in the same kind of small bottle that vanilla extract comes in and can be found in the spice section at just about any supermarket. The reason is that melted real butter is still too thick to get through a spray bottle. Don't worry, though, one ounce of the imitation stuff, which is just soybean oil, won't kill you. Now, the one rule about spritzing your ribs is that you must get the color just right on them *before* you start spritzing, or else you're going to end up washing your bark off—and obviously you don't want that.

Rib Spritz

I use this rib spritz on spareribs and baby back ribs. It's easy to make, and it will change the way your ribs look and taste. You can make it up to a day in advance and store it in the spray bottle, unrefrigerated. Since I can't do that at a contest, I prepare it right after I put my ribs in the smoker. After the ribs have smoked for about 45 minutes, I start spritzing the meat at 15-minute intervals.

Makes about 5 cups

3 cups apple juice
2 cups white wine vinegar
2 tablespoons liquid imitation butter

In a large spray bottle (one that will hold at least 5 cups of liquid), combine all the ingredients. Shake well to blend.

St. Louis Ribs

St. Louis–style ribs do very well in KCBS contests, and because they're larger they tend to be a little bit easier to handle. A lot of folks favor them because they're surrounded by more fat to flavor the meat, and when they're cooked right, they're tender and bursting with real hog flavor.

I cook four racks of ribs at competition, so that's what these recipes call for; that should serve a nice-size group of people, depending on appetites and on what else is on your menu. If you're going to cook fewer ribs, you'll still need to make the rub, marinade, and glaze. You can either cut those recipes in half or you can save the leftovers and use them on other meats (the rib rub, for example, would be great on a pork loin roast), and I'm sure I don't have to tell you what you can do with leftover glaze (I like mine on burgers, though). Regardless of how many racks you're cooking, the cook time stays the same.

Serves 8 to 12

4 racks spareribs
1 recipe Rib Marinade (page 21)
3 cups Jack's Old South Original Rub, or 1 recipe Basic Barbecue Rub (page 20)
1 recipe Rib Spritz (page 73)
1 cup apple juice
1 recipe Hog Glaze (page 23)

What you'll need:
A cutting board
Sharp boning knife or paring knife
Paper towels or clean kitchen towels

One at a time, place the slabs of spareribs on the cutting board, bone side down. Trim off the excess fat from the first three ribs. Turn the slab over. Peel off the thick membrane (or "silver," as it's sometimes called) that covers the ribs. This silver prevents rubs and other seasonings from adhering to the rib rack and doesn't allow a marinade or smoke to penetrate the meat, so it's important to get rid of it. The easiest way to remove the membrane is by making a small incision just below the length of the breastbone. Work your fingers underneath the membrane until you have 2 to 3 inches cleared. Grab the membrane with a towel (which just gives you a better purchase on it) and gently but firmly pull it away from the ribs. Pulling off the membrane exposes loose fat that will need trimming, so take your knife and cut out any excess fat.

The last step is doing the "St. Louis cut," which ensures that the ribs will be uniform in size. Use your boning knife to separate the ribs from the breastbone: Pick the longest bone near the breastbone and use it as a guideline of where to make a horizontal cut along the length of the slab. You should end up with two slabs of ribs that are 5 or 6 inches in length. They won't be curved like the baby backs—that's not how these bones are; they're straight up.

After the ribs are properly trimmed, set the racks in an aluminum baking pan and cover them completely with the rib marinade. Cover the pan with aluminum foil and let it sit for 4 hours, either in the refrigerator or, if you're at a contest or in a picnic situation, in a cooler packed with ice.

When you are ready to cook them, remove the ribs from the marinade. Pat them dry with towels. Apply the rub lightly around the edges of the ribs, over the back side of them, and on top. Then let the ribs sit, uncovered, at room temperature for 30 minutes.

In the meantime, heat a smoker to 275°F.

Put the ribs in a baking pan, put it in the smoker, and cook for 3 hours. After the first 45 minutes of cooking, spritz the ribs. Continue to spritz at 15-minute intervals for the duration of the cooking time. (The ribs should be uncovered so they can absorb as much smoke as possible.)

Remove the pan from the smoker. Pour the apple juice into a clean aluminum pan. Place the ribs in the pan, bone side down, and cover the pan with aluminum foil. Place the pan in the smoker and cook for 2 hours.

Remove the pan from the smoker and shut off the heat on the smoker. Remove the foil, and apply the glaze to the top and bottom of the slabs of ribs. Re-cover the pan with foil, return it to the smoker, and let the ribs rest in the smoker for 1 hour as the temperature gradually decreases.

Remove the ribs from the pan and let them rest for 10 minutes on a wooden cutting board. Then cut and serve.

Baby Back Ribs

My favorite rib to cook and eat is the baby back, because I learned competitive cooking at MIM contests and that's their rib of choice. I just developed a real love for them. They're fun to cook and fun to eat, and they almost always earn me money. Even I can't ask for more than that!

Serves 4 to 6

4 racks baby back ribs
1 recipe Rib Marinade (page 21)
3 cups Jack's Old South Original Rub,
    or 1 recipe Basic Barbecue Rub
    (page 20)
1 recipe Rib Spritz (page 73)
1 cup apple juice
1 recipe Hog Glaze (page 23)

What you'll need:
Cutting board
Sharp boning knife or paring knife
Paper towels or clean kitchen towels

One at a time, place the racks on a cutting board, bone side up, and remove the membrane (or "silver"): At whichever end of the rack seems easier, work your fingers underneath the membrane until you have 2 to 3 inches cleared. Grab the membrane with a towel and gently but firmly pull it away from the ribs. Pulling off the membrane exposes loose fat that will need trimming, so take your knife and cut out any excess fat. Now the racks are ready.

Set the racks in an aluminum baking pan and cover them completely with the rib marinade. Cover the pan with aluminum foil and let it sit for 4 hours, either in the refrigerator or, if you're at a contest or in a picnic situation, in a cooler packed with ice.

When you are ready to cook them, remove the ribs from the marinade. Pat them dry with towels. Apply the rub lightly around the edges of the ribs, over the back side of them, and on top. Then let the ribs sit, uncovered, at room temperature for 30 minutes.

In the meantime, heat a smoker to 250°F.

Put the ribs in a baking pan, put the pan in the smoker, and cook for 2 hours. After the first 30 minutes of cooking, spritz the ribs. Continue to spritz at 15-minute intervals for the duration of the cooking time. (The ribs should be uncovered so they can absorb as much smoke as possible.)

Remove the pan from the smoker. Pour the apple juice into a clean aluminum baking pan. Place the ribs in the pan, bone side down, and cover the pan with aluminum foil. Place the pan in the smoker and cook for 1 hour.

Remove the pan from the smoker and shut off the heat on the smoker. Remove the foil, and apply the glaze to the top and bottom of the slabs of ribs. Re-cover the pan with foil, return it to the smoker, and let the ribs rest in the smoker for 30 minutes as the temperature gradually decreases.

Remove the ribs from the pan and let them rest for 10 minutes on a wooden cutting board. Then cut and serve.

Beef Ribs

When you're talking cow, there are the short ribs (which are good) and there are the back ribs, the big guys, which are tenderlicious. The reason beef ribs are so tender and succulent is because the rib roast, a prime piece of meat, sits right above this section of ribs. So they're prime, too. Cooking them is second nature to me because they happen to look and act a lot like pork baby backs, except of course they're a lot larger. I don't marinate my beef ribs because they come from one of the most marbled areas of the cow, which means they're loaded with natural flavor already. I like my food to be nicely seasoned, but I never want my seasoning to overpower a meat's inherent flavor; seasoning doesn't ever need to be over the top.

Serves 4

16 beef short ribs, or 8 whole beef ribs
2 tablespoons kosher salt
2 tablespoons coarsely ground black
   pepper
3 tablespoons dark brown sugar
1 teaspoon chili powder

½ teaspoon ground turmeric
½ teaspoon ground coriander
1 teaspoon garlic powder
1 teaspoon onion powder
1 recipe Tangy Sweet Sauce (page 23)

Peel off the thick membrane (or "silver," as it's sometimes called) that covers the back side of each rib: Work your fingers underneath the membrane until you have 2 to 3 inches cleared. Grab the membrane with a towel and gently but firmly pull it away from the rib. Pulling off the membrane exposes loose fat that will need trimming, so take your paring knife and cut out any excess fat. Using a clean kitchen towel or paper towels, pat the ribs dry. Set them aside.

In a medium bowl, combine the salt, pepper, brown sugar, chili powder, turmeric, coriander, garlic powder, and onion powder to form a rub. Coat both sides of each rib with the spice mixture. Place the ribs in a large aluminum baking pan, cover, and refrigerate overnight.

When you are ready to cook the ribs, heat a smoker to 275°F.

Place the pan, uncovered, in the smoker and cook for 2 hours.

Remove the pan from the smoker and pour 2 cups of water into the pan. Cover the pan with aluminum foil, return it to the smoker, and cook for 2 more hours.

Remove the ribs from the pan. Glaze the tops of the ribs (only) with the tangy sweet sauce. Don't overdo on the sauce—use just enough to coat the ribs. Put the pan back in the smoker, uncovered, and cook for 15 minutes.

Remove the pan from the smoker and let the ribs sit, loosely covered, for 10 minutes. Then beef out.

Sausage-Stuffed Pork Chops

A pork chop is just a bone-in slice of the pork loin, which is located beneath a hog's ribs and against its backbone. It's a great piece of meat to sink your teeth into, which is why so many people like a pork chop—but it doesn't have a lot of natural fat. This means that it needs some help in the flavor department. Here's how I do it. It'll be the best pork chop you ever had. No joke.

Serves 4

4 2-inch-thick loin pork chops (each about 1 pound)
1 cup Hog Injection (page 21)
1 pound ground pork sausage

3 cups Jack's Old South Original Rub, or 1 recipe Basic Barbecue Rub (page 20)
1 recipe Tangy Sweet Sauce (page 23)

Place the pork chops in a large aluminum baking pan, and cover with the hog injection. Cover, and marinate in the refrigerator for at least 4 hours or overnight.

When you are ready to cook the pork chops, heat a smoker to 300°F.

Remove the pork chops from the marinade, and discard the marinade. Cut a 2-inch-long slit about 2 inches deep in the side of each chop opposite the bone, making a pocket. Remove the pork sausage from the casing, and stuff the sausage deep into the pocket of each pork chop. For each pork chop, use three toothpicks to close off the pocket and hold the sausage in place. Season both sides of each chop with the rub. Put the chops in a clean aluminum baking pan, place the pan in the smoker, and cook for 30 minutes.

Remove the pan from the smoker, flip the pork chops, and return the pan to the smoker. Cook for 30 more minutes.

Remove the pan from the smoker. Glaze the chops on both sides with the tangy sweet sauce, return them to the smoker, and cook for 10 minutes.

Remove the pan and let the chops rest, loosely covered, for 10 minutes. Then serve them up.

Rack of Lamb

Something a south Georgia boy doesn't eat much is lamb. But south Georgia boys who like to win barbecue contests have to figure out how to cook it. The first mutton contest I ever entered I won, cooking lamb chops just like this. I like to get the largest rack of chops I can find, so I can serve them at least an inch thick and give my guests something they can sink their teeth into.

Serves 8

4 1- to 1½-pound racks of lamb, trimmed of all but a ¼-inch layer of fat and frenched (each rack should have 8 ribs)
2 cups dry red wine
½ cup Worcestershire sauce
2 tablespoons distilled white vinegar

1 tablespoon salt
2 tablespoons sugar
3 cups Jack's Old South Original Rub, or 1 recipe Basic Barbecue Rub (page 20)
1 recipe Tangy Sweet Sauce (page 23)

Using a clean kitchen towel or paper towels, pat the racks of lamb dry.

In a large aluminum baking pan, combine the wine, Worcestershire sauce, vinegar, salt, and sugar. Submerge the racks of lamb in the mixture and marinate them, covered, in the refrigerator overnight.

When you are ready to cook the lamb, heat a smoker to 325°F.

Remove the lamb from the marinade, and discard the marinade. Season each rack lightly with the rub. (Season them very lightly so the ribs aren't overly salty.) Place the racks in a clean aluminum baking pan, place the pan in the smoker, and cook for 25 minutes.

Remove the pan from the smoker and glaze the racks with the tangy sweet sauce. Put the pan back into the smoker and cook for 5 additional minutes. Remove the pan and let rack rest for 10 minutes. Then gnaw down.

6

Did you ever see the customers in health-food stores? They are pale,
skinny people who look half dead. In a steak house, you see robust,
ruddy people. They're dying, of course, but they look terrific.
—Bill Cosby

WHAT I LIKE TO EAT and what I like to cook, especially in competition, are often different things. Now, I've been around pork my entire life. It is a key component of any barbecue competition and as such it's been the focus of my career. Pork, from whole hog to shoulder and ribs, dominates. I know very well how to cook a pig, so pork's supremacy never bothers me. But, as delicious as it is, I get burned out on pig. At home I like to cook beef, both on and off the smoker. Whether it's a nice thick porterhouse or a hunk of a brisket's burnt end, beef is my favorite meat to eat when I'm in my backyard, and I'd wager heavily—which I don't do unless I'm planning to take somebody's money—that I'm not alone.

On the barbecue circuit, "beef" means "brisket," and it's a category that gives a lot of teams a fit. I grant you that it is a confusing piece of meat for a lot of home cooks, too. It's a big, tough cut and people don't know what to do with it—even though it's popular around the world. Brisket is sacred to the Irish, who brine it and boil it and call it corned beef, and to Koreans, who boil and press it and call it chadolbaegi, and to Germans, who braise it and call it sauerbraten. What I know about brisket is that despite the fact that it's beloved by so many folks, it's included in barbecue competitions because it's the hardest damn cut of meat to cook.

Brisket is tricky because it's dense and tough and has to be cooked just right or it won't taste good at all. The cut comes from part of the cow's shoulder and its first through fifth ribs. And it's actually relatively cheap—about a fifth the cost of a similarly sized piece of prime rib. What's great about brisket is that when it's cooked properly it becomes something altogether better than the sum of its parts—chewy and tender at the same time, and truly delicious. It just took me a while to understand how to cook it.

Nowadays, brisket is not that complicated for me; it's just that there are a bunch of steps that you have to get right along the way. To cook a good brisket, you have to be patient and methodical. Let me repeat that: There's nothing to cooking a good brisket but being patient and methodical. Each stage of the process is important.

Outside of competition barbecue, I like to cook steaks and burgers. A lot of people don't know this, but I actually have a winning burger recipe. Back in the summer of 2004, I was asked to enter a contest as a side event at the Canadian National Barbecue Championships held at a ski lodge restaurant called

Gitcha some of that!

Dusty's in Whistler, British Columbia. They have a barbecue beef sandwich on the menu there, which they're justifiably proud of, and to go along with it they ran a contest for all competitors to come up with a great burger; the winner got some dough, plus his or her winning burger on the menu for a year. Mine won, and it's the all-time bestselling item on their menu and still available to this day. In this chapter, I'm going to share that recipe for the first time along with some of my favorite steak recipes and the essential method for making great brisket.

Perfect Brisket

Because brisket can be tough if not cooked properly, some other barbecue competitors will actually prepare more than one at a competition. I don't want to cook but one brisket when I compete, and I'm sure not going to do a backup brisket at home. One brisket should be all you need to get the job done. Just pay attention to these steps, and read the info in the box on page 92, and you'll have the one the way you want it, too.

Serves 20 to 25

1 15- to 20-pound whole untrimmed brisket, preferably wagyu (see page 92)

What you'll need:
2 aluminum pans
Injector
Blanket

1 recipe Beef Injection and Marinade (page 21)
1 recipe Beef Rub (page 20)

Trim your brisket (see page 92).

Place the brisket, fat side up, in an aluminum baking pan. Inject it by eyeballing 1-inch squares all over the brisket and injecting half of the beef injection in those squares. Flip the brisket over, fat side down, and pour the remaining injection/marinade over the meat. Cover and refrigerate for at least 6 hours or overnight.

Thirty minutes before you are ready to cook the brisket, heat a smoker to 350°F. (You can also use a gas grill, but you'll need to prepare it for smoking—see page 8.)

Remove the brisket from the marinade and discard the marinade. Using your hands, apply the beef rub all over the meat. Place the brisket in a clean aluminum baking pan, place the pan in the smoker, and cook for 2½ hours.

Remove the pan from the smoker and cover it with aluminum foil. Put it back into the smoker and cook for another 1¹/₂ hours or until the temperature in the point end of the meat reaches 205°F.

Remove the pan from the smoker and wrap the pan, still covered with aluminum foil, in a thick blanket. Let it rest at room temperature for 3 to 4 hours.

Unwrap the pan, discard the foil, and remove the brisket, taking care to save the accumulated juices. Set the brisket aside. Strain the juices of all grease, and pour the juices into a medium saucepan. Warm the juices over medium heat, and allow them to come to a simmer. Meanwhile, slice the brisket against the grain; try to make the slices as consistently sized as possible. Place the slices on a warm platter and pour the juices over them. Serve immediately.

Burnt Brisket Ends

Before marinating a whole brisket, remove the fat cap on the bottom of the brisket, from the center of the meat back to the point (the narrow end). After marinating, season this area with the rub as well as the rest of the meat.

Cook the brisket as described above. Wrap it in the blanket and let it rest for 2 hours.

Unwrap the brisket and remove the bottom section. (There is a membrane separating the bottom of the point from the top. Feel this with your blade as you cut.) Clean the fat away from the membrane side of the bottom piece, season with salt and pepper, and place the bottom piece on the smoker. Cook for 2 hours.

Meanwhile, pour the pan drippings into a grease separator, and set aside. Place the top portion of the brisket back in the pan, wrap it in foil, and rewrap it in the blanket.

Remove the burnt end portion from the smoker and cut it into ½-inch cubes.

Place the cubes in a small pan and add the reserved drippings. Cover, and place in the smoker for 30 minutes.

Remove and enjoy.

All About Brisket

The cut: The average size of a whole brisket is about 12 pounds; I like them a little larger, 15 to 20 pounds, so I can feed more people, either at a contest or in my backyard. Butcher shops and groceries usually break the meat down into two pieces: The first, the "flat" cut, comes from nearer to the cow's belly and is more evenly shaped and lean; the second, the "point" cut, comes from near the foreshank and is rounder and fattier but has more flavor. The recipe on page 90 calls for a whole untrimmed brisket, which you may need to order specially from your butcher, but it's worth it. (If you can't get a whole untrimmed brisket or just are too stubborn to order one, you'll end up with a flat cut or a point; either will weigh about 5 pounds and you can still follow this method to cook it, but you'll need to adjust the cooking time.)

The meat: To make a great brisket, you have to start with a great piece of meat. I used to think that brisket was brisket, that I could get one from any supermarket meat case and win. And for a while, I did. Then my scores started slipping and I had to rethink my position. I began shopping around, talking to folks in the know, and I discovered wagyu beef. Wagyu is a type of cattle that has really fine marbling in its meat, which just means that it's got a lot of fat interspersed nicely with the muscle. That gives it the striped red-and-white look, or "marbled" appearance, you see in a butcher case. The meat from wagyu cattle, which were first cultivated in Japan, is known all over the world for having supremely rich flavor and being especially tender and juicy; this is attributed to its grassy diet. In the United States, wagyu beef is ultra-high-quality and expensive, even for a cut like brisket. A lot of people ask me, *Why do you spend all that goddamn dough on it?* I say, *Look at a wagyu next to a mediocre brisket and it's obvious.* It's about an extra $30 for a potential $10,000 payout in a competition, so it's no question to me. Even if you don't get wagyu, you have to pay attention to the quality of the meat. It is the difference between winning and losing, or between having something truly delicious and something just okay. Buy the best you can find and you won't regret it.

How to trim the meat: Before you get started cooking, you have to trim the membrane, that fine silvery-white weblike coating, from the meat. This involves slowly cutting away the layers of sticky white matter from the actual beef, and it can take damn near forever. But if you don't do it right, your meat is going to be tough and gummy instead of tender and juicy. Another reason is that a dry spice rub won't stick to fat, and the spice rub is what creates that crust, or "bark," that surrounds the brisket, so it's doubly important to do a good job trimming the fat off the meat. It's painstaking, but you have to get it done or you ain't going to have a bark.

How to cook it fast: Traditional barbecue cooks are referred to in competition as "stick burners" because they prefer not to use charcoal and lighter fluid; they prefer the wood-fired pits like my dad used when he was coming up. That's the old-fashioned, tried-and-true way to cook brisket, and I'm not going to tell you that there's anything wrong with it. What I *am* going to tell you is that it takes a long time. A lot of teams think I start my fires late. They're the folks who stay up all night cooking their briskets. Well, about that traditional "slow and low" stuff: It's built on the notion that a tough cut of meat ought to be cooked slowly and at a low temperature in order to break down its fibrous toughness. It's not wrong, but I don't do it. I ain't watching a brisket for 18 hours when I can get just as good results in far less time. Instead, I subscribe to what is called "power cooking." I figured out how to cook my brisket hot and fast by using a water pan, injecting my meat, and maintaining my cooker's temperature at a constant 350°F. And that works for me.

How to maintain the temperature: After I take my brisket out of the smoker, I wrap it up in a blanket while it's resting. (This can be any type of heavy blanket, but it better not be one that you want to use again on your bed.) Folks always look at me curiously when I do this, but I've been doing it for years. It started when I ran into a guy at a gas station in Perry, Georgia. He saw my cook rig and came up to me. He said he was from Texas and asked me if I cooked brisket. I told him I did. And he told me that the best way to make it is to wrap it up in a blanket so that the temperature stays nice and consistent while the meat is resting. So I tried it out by using a sleeping bag I still had from when I was a kid and used to camp out with my brother and my friends. It worked like a charm, and to this day I wrap my briskets up in blankets.

How to get a smoke ring: First of all, you need to understand what exactly a smoke ring is before you worry about how to get one on your brisket. It's the thin pink line just under the meat's surface that is formed as a chemical reaction when meat is properly smoked (it's actually nitric acid that builds up on the meat's surface and is then absorbed by the meat, if you need to get technical). Opinions vary on how to get a really good-looking ring, one that's consistent in size all the way around the meat and substantial enough to be visible, but I think it's a combination of the water pan method and a really good application of a rub that has enough salt in it.

Perfect Porterhouse Steak

A porterhouse is a big hunk of a steak that combines two cuts that are separated by a bone: there's the soft, rich tenderloin on one side, and the firm and juicy sirloin on the other. There are two secrets to a great grilled steak: the quality of the meat (see the note about wagyu beef on page 92), and the seared crust that locks in the steak's juices and flavors. You get the crust by cooking the steak over dry heat in a very hot grill or smoker.

Serves 2 to 4

1 porterhouse steak, at least 1 pound
 and at least 1½ inches thick
1 recipe Beef Injection and Marinade
 (page 21)
Salt, to taste
Coarsely ground black pepper, to taste
1 teaspoon onion powder
1 teaspoon garlic powder

For the sauce:
8 tablespoons (1 stick) unsalted butter
1 tablespoon dark brown sugar
1 teaspoon lemon juice
¼ cup ketchup

Using paper towels or a very clean kitchen towel, pat the steak dry. Place the steak in a baking dish, cover it with the beef injection, and marinate at room temperature for 2 hours.

About 30 minutes before you're ready to cook, prepare a smoker or grill; bring the heat to 500°F.

Remove the steak from the marinade, and discard the marinade. Season the steak liberally on both sides with salt and pepper, and sprinkle it with the onion powder and garlic powder.

Place the steak on the grill rack and sear it over direct heat for about 3 minutes per side.

Transfer the steak to a platter and cover with aluminum foil. Let rest for 5 minutes.

Make your steak sauce: Collect ¼ cup of the drippings from the platter. Combine all the sauce ingredients with the reserved drippings in a small saucepan. Heat over medium heat, whisking continuously, until it just comes to a boil. Set aside.

Uncover the steak. The best way to carve the steak is to use a sharp knife to cut the bone out completely (save it someplace safe for yourself for later on), and then cut the meat across the grain in thick diagonal slices. You want each guest to taste some meat from both sides. Pour the sauce over the slices. Knock yourself out.

Prime Rib

A prime rib roast is such a great way to feed a crowd—it's always on my Christmas dinner table. Sure, it's delicious and decadent, but what most people don't know is that it's easy as hell to cook on a smoker or grill. Note that there are two separate cuts that are considered "prime rib": The first cut (ribs 1 through 3) is closer to the loin and thus more tender and less fatty. The second cut (ribs 4 through 7) is closer to the chuck end and is denser and fattier. Ask your butcher for the first cut—it's worth it—and buy the very best quality beef, with the most marbling, that you can afford. The recipe I'm giving here is for a smaller roast, but the same technique (with a slight adjustment on the time—a good rule of thumb is to allow about 30 minutes per pound) can be applied to a prime rib of any size.

Serves 6 to 8

1 well-marbled 3-rib standing rib roast (about 7 pounds)

1 recipe Beef Injection and Marinade (page 21)

Kosher salt or sea salt, to taste

Coarsely ground black pepper, to taste

1½ tablespoons onion powder

1½ tablespoons garlic powder

Pat the roast dry with paper towels or a clean kitchen towel. Place the roast in an aluminum roasting pan, and inject it all over with the beef injection. Refrigerate for at least 6 hours, or overnight for the best results.

When you are ready to cook the roast, heat a smoker to 250°F.

Take the roast out of the pan, and rub the salt, pepper, onion powder, and garlic powder all over it. Put it back in the pan, and put the pan in the smoker. Cook for 5 hours or until the internal temperature reaches 155°F at the center of the roast.

Take the roast out of the smoker. Put it in a clean roasting pan and cover it with aluminum foil. Wrap the pan in a blanket. Let it rest at room temperature for 1 hour.

Unwrap the pan and transfer the roast to a cutting board, reserving the drippings.

In a medium saucepan over medium heat, allow the drippings to simmer for a couple of minutes. Pour the heated drippings over the roast. Carve it, and serve immediately.

Beef Tenderloin

Beef tenderloin is an expensive, delicate cut of meat that has been blessed with a lot of natural flavor. My thinking is that it needs only a little enhancing, not a total makeover. That's why I don't recommended injecting it. Instead I marinate it, just to add some flavor. One last detail: Beef tenderloin is tender to start with, and over-cooking turns it tough. I repeat: Do not overcook this meat. It won't be worth a damn if you do. If rare to medium-rare ain't your bag, move on and cook a sirloin.

Serves 6

1 2¾- to 3-pound beef tenderloin roast
4 cups beef broth
½ cup distilled white vinegar
1 cup (packed) dark brown sugar
1 12-ounce can Coca-Cola

Using a clean kitchen towel or paper towels, pat the tenderloin dry. Mix the broth, vinegar, brown sugar, and Coca-Cola together in a large roasting pan. Submerge the tenderloin in the marinade, cover, and refrigerate overnight.

When are you are ready to cook the tenderloin, heat a smoker to 275°F.

Transfer the tenderloin to a clean aluminum roasting pan (discard the marinade). Put the pan in the smoker, and cook for about 1½ hours, or until the internal temperature at the center of the tenderloin reaches 155°F. Transfer the tenderloin to a cutting board and let it rest for 10 minutes.

Cut the tenderloin crosswise into ½-inch-thick slices, and serve.

Myron Mixon's Prize-Winning Whistler Burger

In 2004, I won a big burger-cooking contest in Whistler, British Columbia, against a bunch of other professional barbecue cooks. "You were shooting to do America's favorite burger better than it's ever been done before, and you definitely pulled it off." That's what Paul Street, the director of food and beverage at Whistler Black-comb, declared when I was named the champion. Part of winning the competition was the honor of your burger appearing on their menu for a year; my burger's been on the menu ever since that day.

My secret is to smoke the burger first, then sear it in a bit of butter afterward to seal in the moisture, create a crust, and add an extra layer of flavor and richness. I just wanted to come up with the best damn burger I could—one that was meaty and juicy and also infused with great smoky flavor. Now cooking burgers in a smoker is a must for me because I love it when the meat is kissed with smoke; if you've never tried it this way, you ought to. That said, you can do the first step in the oven on those days you don't want to fire up a smoker or grill—it will still be delicious, don't you worry. I like generously portioned burgers, and these are half-pounders. Feel free to make them smaller if you like.

Serves 2

1 pound ground beef, the best and
   freshest you can afford
1 1-ounce packet dry ranch dressing mix
1 teaspoon Beef Rub (page 20)
2 tablespoons unsalted butter
2 slices sharp cheddar cheese
2 slices smoked Canadian bacon
Two white hamburger buns

Garnishes:
Mayonnaise
Iceberg lettuce
Ripe tomato slices

Preheat a smoker or oven to 300°F.

In a medium nonreactive bowl, combine the ground beef with the ranch dressing mix and the beef rub. Mix gently with your hands until the spices are just integrated with the beef—be careful not to overwork the meat. Form into 2 patties (or more if you want smaller burgers).

Place the burgers in a shallow aluminum pan and place the pan in the smoker or in the oven. Cook for 15 minutes for medium-rare and up to 30 minutes for medium-well.

Remove the burgers from the smoker or oven and allow them to rest, uncovered, while you melt the butter in a medium skillet over medium heat. When the butter is hot but not smoking, slide the burgers carefully into the skillet, using a spatula. Cook the burgers for about 3 minutes on each side, just until they're seared and a nice crust has formed—be careful not to overcook them. Top them with the slices of cheddar cheese. Slide the burgers onto a platter and let them rest, lightly covered with aluminum foil.

While your burgers are resting, cook the Canadian bacon and toast the buns: In the same medium skillet over medium heat, cook the slices of Canadian bacon for about 2 minutes on each side, until they are lightly crispy. Using a spatula, slide the Canadian bacon onto paper towels to absorb any excess grease.

Toast the buns on a "light" setting in a toaster oven or toaster. Smear the bottom half of each bun with a little mayonnaise. Top with the cheeseburgers, a slice of Canadian bacon, a nice piece of iceberg lettuce, and a slice of ripe tomato. Smear the top of each bun with a little mayonnaise. And that's the best burger you'll ever put in your mouth.

Grilling Burgers

As with nearly all of the recipes in this book, you can use your grill as a smoker. However, if you don't want to take the time to create some smoke to cook these hamburgers, then you can just grill them. They won't have that delicious smoky flavor and won't be as great as the way I do them, but they'll still be damn good.

Prepare a medium-hot fire in your grill.

Place the burgers on the rack directly over the coals. Cover the grill and cook to your desired doneness, 5 to 7 minutes per side for medium-rare.

Top each burger with a slice of cheddar cheese. Transfer them to a platter and let them rest, lightly covered with aluminum foil.

Cook the Canadian bacon, toast the buns, and fill the buns with the burgers and garnishes as described above.

7

Fish

Chance is always powerful. Let your hook always be cast; in the pool where you least expect it, there will be fish.
—Ovid

I**T'S CONVENIENT FOR ME** that people think fish is so wonderful and love to eat it nowadays. It's convenient because I grew up fishing with my father. There is scarcely a photograph of my father in existence that doesn't show him holding up a prize catch, and he had a lot of them. My dad taught me how to barbecue and he loved it, but the real passion in his life was fishing. My dad fished the way I cook in competitions: as if his life depended on it. The man could catch a fish in a raindrop. He made me and my brother go fishing with him every spare moment we had. He took us so much, going fishing with him felt like a job.

Let me put it to you this way: My daddy, Jack Mixon, was the best fisherman to ever wet a hook in the Flint River. The Flint is a gorgeous body of water that runs south through rural western Georgia, and it's one of the most scenic parts of the Apalachicola River System. Instead of soil, its banks are lined with red Georgia clay. All kinds of native river denizens populate it, and indigenous shoal bass and Gulf sturgeon swim its waters.

Growing up in the house of the "Fishing King," as my dad was known, meant eating fish at least once a week. Saturday was always

The results of my very successful fishing trip in 1987.

Naturally, I turned to my smoker. Conventional wisdom might suggest to some people that delicate, flaky meat like the kind that's on most fish wouldn't stand up to the rough, rustic treatment in a smoker. Well, they'd be wrong. Smoked mullet was my first try at breaking my family's fried-fish tradition. It worked beautifully, with the fish picking up the flavor of the smoke but not becoming overpowered by it. Next I tried catfish, and it was delicious, too. Eventually I smoked just about every variety of fresh- and saltwater resident you can think of, and I've come to believe that smoking is not only one of the most primal forms of cooking but is also one of the healthiest ways to prepare fish. There's no grease, no batter, and thus less cholesterol and less fat. If you can grill hot dogs and burgers, you can cook fish on the barbecue, too. It's that easy.

fried-fish day. It could be catfish, bream, white perch, mullet—whatever came from my dad's fish house, we ate it, and we always ate it the same exact style. It was damn tasty, but damn routine, too. Since making my own way in the world and moving out of Jack's shadow, I have expanded my palate to include fish prepared in ways other than coated in meal and fried.

Mullet

If you think I'm talking about the haircut—"business in the front, recreation in the rear"—you best move on to the next recipe. If you know good food, you've probably heard about mullet, which is a fish found worldwide in tropical and coastal waters and abundantly on both coasts of Florida and into Georgia. Mullet is a bony fish with light meat and a stout body—and it's oily, so it takes especially well to absorbing smoke. Any good fishmonger should be able to get you some.

Serves 4

4 5- to 6-ounce mullet fillets, skin on
1½ cups Jack's Old South Original Rub,
   or 1 recipe Basic Barbecue Rub
   (page 20)

1 medium onion, chopped
8 tablespoons (1 stick) unsalted butter,
   cubed

Heat a smoker to 300°F.

Place the fillets, skin side down, in a small aluminum baking pan. Coat the top of the fish with the rub. Cover the fish with the chopped onions and butter cubes. Cook for 30 minutes or until the flesh of the fish is tender.

Remove and enjoy.

Lobster

I may be from a small town in south Georgia, but that doesn't mean I don't enjoy some fancy food, too. And just as I don't expect people to turn their noses up at cheap pork shoulders that are delicious smoked, I don't turn mine up at lobster tails. They're expensive, but, man, are they good—especially if you cook the tails in the smoker. Try it.

Serves 4

4 raw lobster tails, shells on
3 tablespoons olive oil
Salt, to taste
Freshly ground black pepper, to taste

For the salad:
2 tablespoons mayonnaise
Juice of 1 lemon
2 celery stalks, chopped
¼ head iceberg lettuce, shredded

For serving:
8 tablespoons (1 stick) unsalted butter, melted

What you will need:
Kitchen scissors

Heat a smoker to 325°F.

Using kitchen scissors, cut down the middle of the top of the lobster tails until they are nearly split. Pull the shell apart until the meat is exposed. Place in a bowl and season the tails with the olive oil, salt, and pepper; toss to coat. Place the lobster tails in a large aluminum pan, place the pan in the smoker, and cook for about 10 minutes, or until the meat turns completely white and the tails begin to curl up tightly.

Meanwhile, prepare the salad: In a medium bowl, stir the mayonnaise and lemon juice together until blended. Then add the celery and lettuce, and toss. Set aside.

Remove the lobster tails from the smoker. Do not let the tails cool completely or the meat will become tough. Serve immediately with the melted butter for drizzling and the salad on the side.

Salmon

Serves 4

4 6-ounce salmon steaks, each about 2 inches thick
2 tablespoons olive oil
1 cup Jack's Old South Original Rub, or 1 recipe Basic Barbecue Rub (page 20)

3½ cups Jack's Old South Vinegar Sauce, or 1 recipe Basic Vinegar Sauce (page 22)
1 8-ounce jar apricot preserves
½ cup chopped Vidalia or other sweet onion

Heat a smoker to 350°F.

Brush the salmon steaks with the oil, and sprinkle both sides with the rub. Place them in an aluminum baking pan, put the pan in the smoker, and cook for 10 minutes.

While the fish is cooking, make the glaze: Combine the vinegar sauce, apricot preserves, and chopped onion in a blender, and mix well until thoroughly pureed, about 3 minutes. Pour into a saucepan. Over medium heat, bring the glaze almost to a boil. Remove from the heat.

Remove the pan from the smoker, flip the salmon steaks over, and return the pan to the smoker. Cook for another 5 minutes.

Remove the pan from the smoker and glaze the salmon with the sauce. Serve.

Prawns

Prawns are crustaceans similar to shrimp, but they're a little bit different (it has to do with the number of overlapping plates on their scales, if you want to get technical). That said, the names are used pretty much interchangeably. To me, prawns are a little meatier and sweeter, so if you can get your hands on some, great. If not, substitute the best jumbo shrimp you can find.

Serve these over a bed of wild rice, if you like.

Serves 6

24 prawns or jumbo shrimp, heads on, peeled and deveined, tails intact
3 cups Jack's Old South Original Rub, or 1 recipe Basic Barbecue Rub (page 20)

½ cup lemon juice
½ cup Jack's Old South Hickory Sauce or Basic Hickory Sauce (page 22)
2 tablespoons honey
4 tablespoons (½ stick) unsalted butter

Heat a smoker to 350°F.

Apply the rub to the prawns and place them on skewers. Place the skewers in a large aluminum pan, put the pan in the smoker, and cook for 10 minutes.

While the prawns are cooking, combine the lemon juice, hickory sauce, honey, and butter in a medium saucepan over medium heat. Bring the sauce almost to a boil, and then take the pan off the heat.

Brush the prawns with the sauce, and serve.

Trout

Trout is a freshwater fish, the majority of which swim in the rivers of Idaho and North Carolina. Because it's so commonly farmed, trout is available in markets year-round. It's a meaty fish with a naturally salty flavor, and it takes well to smoking. I like to eat smoked trout as a main dish with a little garlic butter on top and some cheese biscuits on the side. It's also really good in a sandwich with some horseradish, or mixed into a dip with a little mayonnaise and sour cream.

Serves 10

½ cup kosher salt
2 pounds trout fillets (3 to 5 ounces each), skin on, pin bones removed

Combine the salt and 4 cups water in a 4-quart container and stir until the salt has dissolved, 1 to 2 minutes. Submerge the trout fillets in the mixture, cover, and refrigerate for 3 hours.

Remove the trout from the brine, rinse them thoroughly, and pat dry. Place the trout, skin side down, on a rack set in a baking pan. Place the pan in the refrigerator and leave, uncovered, for about 24 hours or until the skin is shiny and sticky to the touch.

When you are ready to cook the trout, heat a smoker to 160°F.

Place the trout fillets in an aluminum pan, skin side down, separating them by at least ¼ inch. Place the pan in the smoker and cook for 2½ to 3 hours, or until the fish is cooked through and darkened in color.

Remove trout from smoker and serve immediately.

At seventeen, catching bream with my dad.

8

Side Dishes

You don't win friends with salad.
—Homer Simpson

SOME PEOPLE WILL TELL YOU that nobody really cares about the main courses, and that side dishes are where it's at. I say that those people must be vegetarians, or else they've been traumatized by some really bad Thanksgiving turkeys. I'm not going to pretend that barbecue is about anything but meat, because for me it is. The smoked meat is the star of every picnic and backyard party and competitive barbecue event in the world. But everybody knows that man—and woman, for that matter—cannot live by meat alone. That's why God invented side dishes, isn't it?

Side dishes were important to barbecue when I was growing up. When I think back, I remember my granny grinding the pork and onions for the Brunswick stew she was getting ready to make for the family barbecue dinner. It's true that traditional Southern side dishes such as potato salad, coleslaw, and baked beans really enhance the meat. If you want to get technical about it, they add flavor dimensions to the plate that complement the smoke and sweetness of the big draw. You want the side dishes to help the meat shine; when they're cooked right, they make up the supporting cast you need at any good barbecue.

You know I wouldn't pay too much more attention to side dishes if there wasn't a way to get paid for them. Some barbecue contests actually have side dish categories. It will come as no surprise to you by this point that I like to win money, so I had to not only appreciate side dishes but get good at cooking them, too. I've won for baked beans at several contests. The thing to remember is that any of the contests that aren't strictly devoted to barbecue are not vetted by certified barbecue judges. The judges are often the VIP sponsors of the contest or some local politicians or some people like that. So you need to make sure you are cooking for the masses. When you're throwing a party at home, it's the same thing. I say stick with what most people eat and like. You don't have to reinvent the wheel when it comes to side dishes. The classics got to be that way for a reason.

For example, take baked beans. When I was trying to figure out a good recipe for them, I thought about what baked beans ought to taste like. I knew some people did not care for baked beans, but there aren't many true Americans who don't like pie. That's why I use peach pie filling in my beans. Those are proven flavors that almost everybody likes. I try to think that way with all my side dishes. They are dependable classics, and they make the meat look and taste damn good.

Myron's Peach Baked Beans

I always try to make any food taste good by preparing it as simply as possible. This comes from the original idea of how barbecue was started and why it has become so popular: It's a way to cheaply and efficiently feed a lot of people some tasty food. My beans recipe is no different. I keep it simple and focus on enhancing the flavors that people have come to love and expect in baked beans. I'm not trying to fool anybody here: baked beans are a barbecue staple. And some people just don't like them at all because they tend to be sweet. In other words, I'm not trying to convert anybody with this recipe; I'm preaching to the converted. This is my take on how classic baked beans always ought to taste.

Note that you have to soak your beans overnight to get them tender; some people say you don't, but I believe it's the only way to really make sure they're going to taste right. If time is an issue, you can substitute canned baked beans in this recipe; personally, I think they taste great, too.

Serves 8

2 pounds (about 4 cups) dried navy or
   great northern beans
¼ cup (packed) light brown sugar
Salt and freshly ground black pepper,
   to taste
¼ cup prepared mustard

¼ cup maple syrup
½ cup ketchup
3 cups canned peach pie filling
1 7-ounce jar diced pimento peppers,
   drained

Place the beans in a large nonreactive bowl, and add enough cold water to cover them by 3 to 4 inches. Cover the bowl loosely with a kitchen towel and leave the beans to soak at room temperature overnight.

When you are ready to cook the beans, rinse them thoroughly in fresh cold water, and drain.

Place the beans in a large pot, and add water to cover. Bring to a boil, reduce the heat, and simmer for 1 hour. Drain the beans.

Preheat a smoker or oven to 300°F.

In a large bowl, combine the brown sugar, salt and pepper, mustard, maple syrup, ketchup, pie filling, and peppers. Mix well. Then add the beans and stir again. Pour the bean mixture into a large aluminum pan (for the smoker) or into a large ovenproof baking dish or Dutch oven. (You can assemble the beans to this point 1 day ahead; cover and refrigerate until you're ready to cook them.)

Add just enough water to the pan to cover everything, and cover the pan with aluminum foil. Cook in the smoker or oven until the beans are tender, about 4 hours, checking hourly to make sure they aren't drying out (if they are, add more water to the pan). The beans are done when the top is dark brown and bubbling. If you want the top to be slightly crunchy, uncover the pan for the last 30 minutes of cooking.

Let the beans stand for about 15 minutes, then serve.

Zesty Potato Salad

On the second season of *Pitmasters,* I wasn't a competitor; I was a judge. What can I say—that's what happens when no one can beat you. Anyway, the judging panel consisted of football star Warren Sapp, chef Art Smith, and yours truly. On one episode, we held a competition for the best homemade potato salad. I pride myself on my potato salad. I said to the contestants, "You got to have mayonnaise to have a good potato salad." I don't care what else you put in it—it's got to be a little bit creamy.

Serves 8

2 pounds red-skinned new potatoes
1 cup sour cream
1 teaspoon dried dill weed
½ teaspoon garlic powder
½ teaspoon onion powder
⅓ cup chopped fresh chives
1 cup mayonnaise

1 tablespoon coarsely ground black
   pepper
1 tablespoon salt
6 hard-boiled eggs, chopped
Basic Barbecue Rub (page 20),
   for garnish (optional)

Wash the potatoes well. In a large heavy pot, bring water to a boil. Add the potatoes and boil for 15 to 20 minutes, or until they are tender, being careful not to overcook them, as you don't want them mushy.

Drain the potatoes in a colander, and run cold water over them to stop them from continuing to cook. Let them cool in the colander.

Slice the potatoes into thin rounds, leaving the skin on. Set aside.

In a medium bowl, combine the sour cream, dill, garlic powder, onion powder, chives, mayonnaise, pepper, and salt. Stir well.

In a large bowl, toss the potatoes with the chopped eggs and the sour cream dressing. Cover the bowl and chill in the refrigerator for 2 hours before serving. Sprinkle top with basic barbecue rub before serving, if desired.

Mama's Slaw

Coleslaw is an extremely time-honored side dish that is served with all sorts of things in the South. *Cole* is actually an old English word for "cabbage," which is of course what coleslaw is always made out of. This is my very favorite coleslaw recipe. In the South, creamy slaws like this one are traditional with fish dinners, and this is the slaw we always serve at our fish fries. It is served cold and smooth and is just perfect with fried fish and hushpuppies. Vinegar-based slaw is the classic to go with barbecue, but this one happens to taste great with barbecued meats, too.

Serves 12

2 small heads green cabbage, coarsely chopped
2 medium sweet onions, diced
2 ripe tomatoes, diced

3 cups mayonnaise
Kosher salt, to taste
Freshly ground black pepper, to taste
Basic Barbecue Rub (page 20), optional

In a large bowl, combine the cabbage, onions, tomatoes, mayonnaise, salt, and pepper. Toss thoroughly. (You can prepare this up to 6 hours in advance and store it, covered, in the refrigerator. But if you do, do not add the salt until you're ready to serve the slaw, and toss it again just before serving; otherwise, the slaw becomes watery.) Garnish with basic barbecue rub, if desired.

Serve immediately.

Cracklin' Cornbread

Cornbread is *the* Southern starch; it's been in the South as long as there have been cooks to make it. Some people I know still call it corn pone. I always cook it in a well-seasoned cast-iron skillet and add my secret ingredient: cracklin's. These are fried pieces of pork skin, and they are incredibly delicious; they're the by-product of rendering pig skin for fat, and because I cook a lot of whole hogs I have the makings for them around all the time. If you don't, feel free to substitute some nice crispy bacon instead. You might also add some chopped red bell pepper for a change and some color.

Serves 6

1 cup all-purpose flour
1 cup yellow cornmeal
1 teaspoon salt
1 egg, beaten

1 cup milk
1 cup chopped crisp pork cracklin's
    (see page 60) or crumbled crisp
    bacon

Preheat the oven to 425°F.

In a large mixing bowl, sift the flour, cornmeal, and salt together until thoroughly combined. Add the egg and the milk, and mix until the batter is relatively smooth. Add the pork cracklin's. If the mixture seems too dry, add a tablespoon or two of water to moisten it.

Pour the batter into an 8-inch cast-iron skillet or an 8-inch square baking pan. Bake until the top is golden brown and a tester inserted into the middle of the cornbread comes out clean, 20 to 25 minutes.

Remove the cornbread from the oven and allow it to cool in the pan for 10 minutes before cutting and serving.

Layered Salad with Potato Sticks

There's no better side dish for a barbecue on a hot summer's day than this layered salad, which is sweet and salty all at once. If you like Hawaiian pizza, with bacon and pineapple on it, this salad is for you.

Serves 6

1 head iceberg lettuce

6 slices bacon, cooked and chopped, or
    1 4.1-ounce can bacon bits

4 hard-boiled eggs, chopped

1 cup diced fresh pineapple, or
    1 8-ounce can pineapple niblets,
    drained

¼ cup chopped green onions (scallions),
    white and green parts

1 cup grated sharp cheddar cheese

1 cup mayonnaise

1 cup sugar

1 cup canned or bagged shoestring
    potato sticks

¾ cup dried cranberries or cherries

Cut the head of lettuce into bite-size pieces.

In a large serving bowl, and in this order, layer the lettuce, chopped bacon, chopped eggs, pineapple, green onions, and cheese. Set aside.

In a small bowl, stir the mayonnaise and sugar together until well combined.

Drizzle the mayonnaise mixture over the salad. Scatter the potato sticks and cranberries on top of the dressing. Chill the salad, covered, for 1 hour before serving.

Brunswick Stew

When I make this stew, an extremely old-fashioned and indigenous example of the "poor people" food that the South was built on, I feel like I'm cooking a piece of my own history. The origins of this piquant, thin stew, which is loaded with meat and vegetables, are hotly disputed between Brunswick, Georgia, and Brunswick County, Virginia (I'm a Georgia product myself, so you know which side I'm on). I always make this for a crowd. A big crowd. Like those at my cooking school, which typically draws more than fifty students. I have my own professional-size meat grinder, and what I often do is grind the onions and potatoes together with the pork and brisket. You don't need to do that at home; you can just mix them together. And feel free to cut this recipe in half (or quarters, whatever you need), but I suggest you make it for your next snow day, and bake up some cornbread to go with it—feed the whole block and you'll have friends for life, trust me.

Serves 50

7 pounds potatoes, peeled and quartered
   or coarsely chopped
3 pounds yellow onions, quartered
3 pounds Pork Shoulder (page 57),
   finely shredded
3 pounds Brisket (page 90), finely
   shredded

1 cup sugar
7 pounds canned crushed tomatoes
7 pounds canned creamed corn
7 pounds canned tomato sauce
2 cups Jack's Old South Vinegar Sauce,
   or 1 recipe Basic Vinegar Sauce
   (page 22)

Preheat the oven to 300°F.

Combine the potatoes, onions, meats, sugar, canned vegetables, tomato sauce, and vinegar sauce in a very large roasting pan or two medium roasting pans. Cover the pan(s) with aluminum foil, place in the oven, and cook, stirring frequently and making sure no meat sticks to the bottom of the pan, for 4 hours or until the onions are thoroughly cooked. Serve warm, in bowls.

Stuffed Pear Salad

Cold fruit salads like this one are an old-fashioned piece of Americana. You can find recipes for stuffed canned peaches and pears and other so-called salads like this one in historic Southern cookbooks and of course in classics like the *Joy of Cooking* and *The Settlement Cookbook.* You don't see them much around anymore, which is a shame because this salad is cool and refreshing—a great thing to serve for a summer lunch or as a first course for a dinner party. It may seem weird nowadays to serve canned pears with mayo, but would I waste my time with something that wasn't good as hell? I didn't think so.

Serves 6

1 16-ounce can pear halves, drained
¼ cup mayonnaise
¼ cup shredded sharp cheddar cheese

6 cherries, fresh (pitted) or maraschino
12 to 18 large iceberg lettuce leaves, rinsed and dried

Place pear halves, cut side up, on a plate. Spoon about 2 teaspoons of the mayonnaise into the cavity of each pear. Sprinkle the cheese over the mayonnaise. Top each one with a cherry. Chill the pears, covered, for at least 3 hours.

To serve, arrange 2 to 3 lettuce leaves on a plate and place the pear halves on top of them.

Barbecue Deviled Eggs

Deviled eggs remind me of church picnics and Fourth of July parties and just about every occasion I grew up going to where there was food involved. Of course I make my own deviled eggs, but you know I'm not going to make them like everybody else's; I put my own stamp on them. And that means barbecue. Deviled eggs stuffed with a little of it makes them better than you've ever had them, I promise you that.

Makes 14

7 large eggs, hard-boiled and peeled
¼ cup mayonnaise
1½ tablespoons sweet pickle relish
1 cup finely pulled Pork Shoulder
   (page 57), smoked Chicken (page 40),
   or Brisket (page 90), chopped

Salt and freshly ground black pepper, to
   taste
2 to 3 tablespoons Jack's Old South
   Original Rub or Basic Barbecue Rub
   (page 20)

Halve the eggs lengthwise. Cut a small slice from the bottom of each half so the egg will lie flat on a platter or in a deviled egg dish.

Remove the yolks and place them in a small bowl. Mash the yolks with a fork. Stir in the mayonnaise, pickle relish, meat, and salt and pepper. Mix well. Spoon the yolk mixture back into the egg white "cups." Sprinkle a little of the rub over each egg.

Serve immediately, or cover and refrigerate for up to 4 hours until ready to serve.

9

Myron at Home

*I don't like gourmet cooking or "this" cooking or "that" cooking.
I like good cooking.*
—James Beard

AFTER *PITMASTERS,* THE TELEVISION SHOW that I'm featured on, developed something of a following, people started recognizing me at competitions for more than the fact that I am almost always on the winners' podium. They now know me as "that guy on TV." In fact, sometimes in competitions people come up to my rig just to try to get me to say something nasty, something that would make my momma, who is a God-fearing woman and always has been, want to wash my mouth out with soap. ("My wife just wants to wash your mouth out with soap," a fan of the show came up to me one time and said. "I'll let her if you pay me," I replied.) Sometimes folks even come up to me just to tell me that they hate me. I like that, actually. It makes me want to keep winning even more.

The one thing, though, that people probably ask me the most is what I like to eat besides barbecue. I guess it's only natural, because I am an expert in this field, that people might assume that all I eat is 'cue. I don't, of course. Hell, even the Lord took a day off, didn't he?

The truth is that I like all kinds of food, so long as it's good. Some of the most fun I have at competitions is coming up with original recipes for the ancillary portions, which are those that run alongside the traditional barbecue contests and are all about cooking stuff such as my catfish-shrimp alfredo, which has become one of my own personal signature dishes. I'm proud to say I've won a whole bunch of ancillaries, which is proof that I can cook more than "just barbecue."

That said, almost all of the food I truly love and gravitate toward is simple stuff: good ingredients, strong flavors, and easy preparation. I don't mind telling you that I love chicken livers wrapped in bacon, because I defy anyone to say they're not delicious. You want to step into my world of food outside of the rig? Come check it out.

Bacon-Wrapped Chicken Livers

One of my favorite at-home foods is this appetizer/snack, which I love to munch on while I'm cooking out in my backyard. These are great with cocktails and addictive as hell. They're easy to throw together and put in the smoker alongside whatever else you may already be cooking in there.

Serves 4 to 6 as an appetizer

8 ounces sliced bacon
1 pound chicken livers
1 cup Jack's Old South Huney Muney
    Cluck Rub, or 1 recipe Basic Chicken
    Rub (page 20)

1½ cups Jack's Old South Hickory
    Sauce, or 1 recipe Basic Hickory
    Sauce (page 22)

Heat a smoker to 325°F.

Cut each bacon slice in half crosswise. Set the slices aside.

Rinse the chicken livers and pat them dry. Lightly prick each one with a fork to prevent popping. Sprinkle the livers with the chicken rub. Wrap each liver in a bacon strip, and secure it with a toothpick. Place the wrapped chicken livers in a medium-size aluminum pan.

Place the pan in the smoker and cook for approximately 10 minutes, or until the bacon is thoroughly cooked.

Remove the pan from the smoker and glaze the livers thoroughly with the hickory sauce. Munch.

Lamb Shoulder

Mutton is a lamb's older brother; lambs are less than a year old and are tender, while mutton has a stronger smell and a more intense game flavor. They love mutton in western Kentucky; it's the traditional meat that's barbecued there, and I know this because a few years ago I won the Kentucky state mutton championship cooking that very thing. My secret is treat it like a pork butt with an attitude. Note that this ain't lamb chops: you've got to inject the meat and cook it for a while to get it tender. It's worth it. One tip: Don't put damn mint jelly on this meat. My Tangy Sweet Sauce is the only way to go.

Serves 6

1 2½- to 3-pound boneless lamb
   shoulder
8 cups Hog Injection (page 21)

1 cup apple juice
2 cups Tangy Sweet Sauce (page 23)

Place the lamb shoulder in a large aluminum roasting pan. Inject the meat all over with the hog injection, making sure to inject the marinade slowly and carefully and not to make too many holes in the meat. Cover, and let the meat sit in the refrigerator for at least 3 hours or overnight.

When you are ready to cook the meat, heat a smoker to 275°F.

Place the roasting pan, uncovered, in the smoker and cook for 2 hours. Remove the pan from the smoker and pour in the apple juice. Cover the pan with aluminum foil, put it back in the smoker, and cook for about 2 more hours or until the internal temperature of the shoulder is 175°F.

Uncover the pan and let the lamb rest for 10 minutes. Then transfer it to a cutting board and slice. Serve the tangy sweet sauce alongside for dipping.

Fried Catfish

Serves 8

Vegetable or canola oil, for deep-frying
8 5- to 6-ounce catfish fillets, skin
   removed
Salt, to taste

Crab boil seasoning, such as Old Bay,
   to taste
4 cups all-purpose flour
1 cup yellow cornmeal

Fill a deep-fryer or a deep pot halfway with oil, and heat it to 350°F.

Sprinkle both sides of the catfish fillets with salt and crab boil seasoning.

In a bowl, combine the flour and the cornmeal. Dredge the catfish in the flour mixture.

Carefully place the fillets in the hot oil, and deep-fry for 7 to 8 minutes, or until golden. Remove and drain on paper towels. Serve immediately.

Lowcountry Boil

When I host cooking school weekends at my place, I often do a Lowcountry Boil on Friday nights for my usual "meet and greet" session, where the folks attending can get to know one another—and me—a little bit. This is a specialty of the Lowcountry areas like Charleston and Savannah, where the people live near the water and have access to plenty of fresh shrimp. But of course you don't need to live near the water to enjoy it. The traditional way to serve this is to basically dump it—spread it, if you will—across a large picnic table that has been covered with newspaper. You may want to fancy up the serving situation, but it's fine to keep it casual, too. You can just tell your guests that's how they do it down South.

Serves 8 to 10

2 to 2½ pounds fully cooked smoked sausage, cut into 1-inch pieces
¼ cup Old Bay Seasoning, or more to taste
16 to 20 small new potatoes
8 to 10 ears corn, shucked, silk removed, ears broken in half

4 to 5 pounds large fresh shrimp (16-to-20-count size), shell on
3 tablespoons salt

For serving:
Tartar sauce
Cocktail sauce
3 lemons, quartered

Fill a large pot with enough water to cover all the ingredients, and bring to a boil.

Add the sausage and Old Bay Seasoning, and boil for about 20 minutes so the sausage can flavor the water. Carefully taste for seasoning; add more Old Bay if desired.

Add the potatoes and boil for about 15 minutes, until nearly tender. Add the corn and boil for about 10 minutes.

Finally, add the shrimp and cook for 3 minutes or until they are cooked through. Drain immediately and serve on an oversize platter or on a table covered with newspaper. Serve tartar and cocktail sauces, lemon wedges, and a small bowl of salt alongside.

Catfish-Shrimp Alfredo

This dish might sound a little strange coming from me, I grant you that. But you know I wouldn't bother with it if it didn't make me some dough, and the concoction has won me a bunch of money in contest ancillary categories over the years. It's a Myron Mixon original recipe if ever there was one.

Serves 4

3½ cups (7 sticks) salted butter
3 bell peppers, preferably an orange, a red, and a yellow, diced
6 cloves garlic, minced
1 Vidalia or other sweet onion, chopped
3 cups Jack's Old South Original Rub, or 1 recipe Basic Barbecue Rub (page 20)
1½ pounds catfish, cut into 4 pieces, each about 8 inches in length, *or* 4 catfish fillets (1½ pounds total)
4 cups chicken broth

1 cup orzo pasta
1 cup quick-cooking wild rice
16 large shrimp, peeled and deveined
2 cups heavy cream
1 cup freshly grated Parmigiano-Reggiano cheese
Freshly ground black pepper, to taste
1 16-ounce can salad shrimp, drained
1 6-ounce can crabmeat, drained and picked free of any broken shells

Heat a smoker to 250°F.

In a large skillet over medium-high heat, melt 2 sticks of the butter. Add all but a handful (which you'll use as a garnish) of the bell peppers to the pan and cook until they soften, about 3 minutes. Add 4 more sticks of butter, the garlic, and the onion. Sauté together until the onion is soft and translucent, about 5 minutes. Take the pan off the heat and set it aside.

Apply some of the rub to both sides of the fish fillets. Put the fillets on a large flat aluminum pan, place it in the smoker, and cook for 5 minutes. Remove the pan from the smoker, flip the fish over, and cook for 5 more minutes.

Remove the pan from the smoker and transfer the fish to a large cast-iron skillet or other pan. Pour the bell pepper–onion-butter sauce over the fillets. Cover the skillet with aluminum foil and place it in the smoker. Cook for 10 minutes. Then remove the skillet and let the fish rest, still covered.

While the fish is cooking, bring the chicken broth to a boil in a large pot. Add the orzo and cook for 5 minutes. Then add the wild rice and cook until the orzo is just done, about 5 minutes. Cover the pot and set it aside, off the heat.

Apply the remaining rub to the shrimp. Place them on a flat aluminum pan, put the pan in the smoker, and cook for 10 minutes.

While the shrimp are cooking, make the alfredo sauce: Heat the heavy cream in a deep sauté pan over medium-low heat. Add the remaining 1 stick butter and whisk gently to melt. Sprinkle in the cheese and stir to incorporate. Season with freshly ground black pepper to taste. Stir the salad shrimp and crabmeat into the sauce. Stir over medium heat until hot.

Stir half of the shrimp-crab sauce into the orzo mixture.

Remove the shrimp from the smoker and let sit in the pan, still covered, until ready to use.

Mound the orzo mixture on four plates. Lay the catfish fillets on top of the orzo mounds. Drizzle the remaining shrimp-crab sauce over the fish, and top that with the smoked shrimp. Garnish with the remaining diced bell peppers.

Meat Loaf

Meat loaf is something every man ought to know how to cook. I developed my recipe when I started having my cooking schools. I always host a Friday night meet-and-greet Lowcountry Boil, but inevitably some of my students don't eat seafood, and for them I created individual meat loaves—kind of like large meatballs made for just one person. Everybody knows the best thing about meat loaf is the sandwiches you can have the next day with the leftovers; these are no different.

Serves 4

2 pounds ground beef
½ sleeve Ritz crackers, crushed
   (about ¾ cup)
1 egg, beaten
¼ cup ketchup
2 slices white bread, lightly moistened
   with water and torn into small pieces
1 medium onion, chopped

Salt and freshly ground black pepper,
   to taste

For the sauce:
¼ cup ketchup
2 teaspoons prepared mustard
3 tablespoons (packed) light brown
   sugar

Preheat the oven to 300°F.

In a large bowl, using your hands, thoroughly combine the beef, crushed crackers, egg, ketchup, bread pieces, onion, and salt and pepper. Form the mixture into 4 mini loaves. Place the loaves in a large baking dish, cover with aluminum foil, and bake for 1 hour.

While the meat is cooking, make the sauce: In a small bowl, combine the ketchup, mustard, and brown sugar. Stir thoroughly.

Remove the baking dish from the oven and spoon all of the sauce over the loaves. Return the dish to the oven and bake, uncovered, for 10 minutes. Serve immediately.

Barbecue Nachos

If you ever find yourself wondering what to do with that last pound of barbecue, I've got a solution for you: nachos. This is the best damn appetizer in the world, especially good for things like Super Bowl parties and poker games. You can make your own salsa, of course, but I usually just use whichever brand I happen to have in the fridge.

Serves 4

1 large bag (about 8 ounces) corn
   tortilla chips
1 pound shredded Pork Shoulder
   (page 57), shredded Chicken
   (page 40), or shredded Brisket
   (page 90)
2 cups shredded sharp cheddar cheese
   (about 6 ounces)

2 cups salsa
3 to 4 pickled jalapeño peppers, thinly
   sliced
Guacamole (optional)
Sour cream (optional)

Preheat the oven to 350°F.

Line a large baking sheet with parchment paper. Spread the chips evenly in one layer across the sheet. Top the chips with the shredded meat, cheese, salsa, and jalapeño slices.

Place the baking sheet in the oven and bake for about 5 minutes to melt the cheese.

Transfer the nachos to individual plates or just slide them off the parchment onto a platter and take that to the table. Serve immediately, with guacamole and sour cream if you like.

Barbecue-Stuffed Baked Potatoes

When my brothers and I were cooking and working at my father's barbecue restaurant, we had barbecue baked potatoes on the menu and they were popular as hell. I ate them for lunch all the time, and to this day I make them whenever I have leftover pulled pork.

Makes 4 main-course or 8 side-dish servings

4 large russet potatoes (about 12 ounces each)
2 tablespoons olive oil
Salt, to taste
¾ cup sour cream (plus more for garnish)
5 tablespoons unsalted butter, at room temperature

Freshly ground black pepper, to taste
1 pound Pork Shoulder (page 57), shredded
½ cup plus 4 teaspoons shredded sharp cheddar cheese
¼ cup chopped green onions (scallions), white and green parts

Preheat the oven to 350°F.

Rinse the potatoes very well under cold water and scrub them clean. Dry them well with a clean kitchen towel. Pierce each potato with the tip of a sharp knife or the tines of a fork (so that steam can escape during baking and the potato doesn't explode). Roll the potatoes in the olive oil and sprinkle them with salt. Bake the potatoes for about 1½ hours. To test for doneness, gently squeeze the potatoes' sides; they should yield nicely to the touch. Remove the potatoes from the oven and let them rest for 5 minutes. Do not turn the oven off.

Cut each potato in half, lengthwise. Using a large spoon, scoop out the insides of the potato halves, leaving enough flesh on the skin so the shell remains intact. Set the potato shells aside. Put the scooped-out potato in a large bowl.

Add the sour cream, butter, and salt and pepper to the bowl, and mash with a fork until the potato filling is combined and smooth. Fold in the pork and ½ cup of the cheese.

Spoon the mixture into the potato shells, and place the shells on a large baking sheet. Bake in the oven for about 15 minutes or until thoroughly warmed through.

Remove the potatoes from the oven, top with the remaining 4 teaspoons cheese and the green onions and sour cream and serve immediately.

Chicken Salad

I love a chicken salad sandwich, but I like the chicken salad itself to be full of flavor and not plain and boring. So when I make chicken salad, I start with a whole chicken because I like both white and dark meat, and because I want to have a lot of chicken salad to go around. Then I put pickles, apples, grapes, eggs, and pecans in it, so that it's a rich, filling salad that's great on its own with Ritz or saltine crackers, or on a toasted English muffin, or on other bread as a sandwich.

Should you have any leftover barbecue chicken (see page 31) or smoked chicken (see page 40), you can scale down this recipe based on what you have and make a smaller amount of the chicken salad with the leftovers.

Serves 6 to 8

1 large whole chicken (4½ to 5 pounds)
9 to 10 cups chicken broth or water
2 cups mayonnaise
½ cup sweet pickle relish
2 cups chopped apples

2 cups halved seedless red grapes
1 cup chopped pecans
8 hard-boiled eggs, chopped
Salt and freshly ground black pepper,
    to taste

Place the chicken and broth in a large pot, cover, and bring to a boil. Reduce the heat and simmer gently until the chicken is cooked through and the meat is ready to fall off the bone, about 45 minutes.

Using tongs, transfer the chicken to a plate; set it aside until it is cool enough to handle. Then pull the meat from the bones in large pieces, discarding the skin and bones.

In a large bowl, combine the chicken with the mayonnaise, relish, apples, grapes, pecans, and eggs. Season with salt and pepper. Mix well. Serve over greens or in a sandwich.

Barbecue Chef Salad

Serves 4

3 cups green-leaf lettuce, rinsed and
    spun dry
3 cups romaine lettuce, rinsed, spun dry,
    and chopped
¼ cup finely diced red onion
¼ cup chopped red bell pepper
3 to 4 pickled jalapeño peppers, sliced
¹/₃ pound pepper jack cheese, grated

1 pound shredded Pork Shoulder
    (page 57), and/or shredded Chicken
    (page 40), and/or shredded Brisket
    (page 90)
2 large eggs, hard-boiled, peeled, and
    cut crosswise into thin slices
1 cup Tangy Sweet Sauce (page 23)

Line four large plates with the green-leaf lettuce.

In a large bowl, combine the romaine lettuce, onion, bell pepper, jalapeño slices, cheese, and meat. Toss well. Mound the salad mixture on the center of the green-leaf lettuces, and arrange the egg slices on top. Drizzle the sauce over the salads. Serve immediately.

Pimiento Cheese

Pimiento cheese is the bright orange spread that Southerners are crazy for because it's comforting and delicious and traditional. It's most often served as a dip or spread, but it's also good in a sandwich all by itself or as a topping on burgers. I like to make up a big batch for family gatherings and barbecues, and if I have some left over, I'll eat it in a sandwich the next day. I'm going to give you a big recipe, too, so you can do the same.

Serves 20

3 cups (about 1½ pounds) grated medium-sharp cheddar cheese

3 cups (about 1½ pounds) grated processed cheese, such as Velveeta

2 4-ounce jars chopped pimiento peppers, with their juice

½ cup sugar

3 cups mayonnaise

2 tablespoons freshly ground black pepper

In a large bowl, mix the cheeses, peppers and juice, sugar, mayonnaise, and black pepper with a metal spoon (the peppers will stain plastic or wood), and stir until the mixture is well blended. Keep covered in the fridge until ready to use. Serve with your favorite crackers, good crusty bread, or corn chips.

10

Drinks and Desserts

The problem with the world is that everyone is a few drinks behind.
—Humphrey Bogart

SOME PEOPLE THINK that because the barbecue world is largely concerned with meat, people like me don't know anything about dessert. I don't know where they get that idea. Dessert is definitely associated with barbecue! Down here, there is always peach ice cream, apple crunch, peach cobbler, banana pudding, grilled peaches . . . We aren't going to miss any opportunity to eat good food, even if it isn't wrapped in pork fat and didn't come off of a hot smoker.

That said, and as you can tell from the sweets I already named, most of the desserts in my world are basic Southern staples. That's probably why a lot of barbecue cookbooks leave them out altogether, either because people don't think these desserts are worth talking about along with the meat or because there are already a lot of other sources for that kind of information. And they have a point, because we barbecue guys are not sitting down here in our backyards whipping up cream puffs and stacking them all together like some big topiary tree the way the French chefs do. That day isn't coming any time soon.

Now don't get me wrong; complicated desserts can be delicious and if someone devotes time and energy to creating them, they're an honest-to-god art form. I get it. But I also believe that there is nothing more delicious in this world than good old-fashioned banana pudding layered with vanilla wafers and topped with meringue. You can keep your French pastries.

Some Southern cooks have too many damned versions of banana pudding, too. I know one woman who must do it ten different ways. That's not my philosophy of cooking at all. I say, if I have one good recipe, why the hell do I need nine more? When I found the best way to make banana pudding, I stuck with it. And I'll share it with you.

The truth is, if you spend any time attending even the most casual of social events in the South, then you're going to be called upon at some point to produce a dessert. There's always going to be a picnic or a potluck or a barbecue with a dessert table that needs a contribution. So I've had to learn, like many cooks before me, how to make a few dessert staples that I can reliably count on to be delicious. If you're one of those people who doesn't like to cook anything that doesn't come off a grill or smoker—and sometimes I'm guilty of feeling that way myself—try my grilled peaches brushed with rum glaze; you don't even need to step inside to make those.

I put drinks in the same chapter with desserts because cocktails and other libations are just as important to enjoying a good barbecue meal as a sweet ending is. During the daytime, and especially when I'm out competing or teaching barbecue classes, I can't get

enough sweet tea. It's the signature drink of the South and is just about perfect with a pulled pork sandwich or a plate of ribs. Some people use barbecue as an excuse to get sloshed, but that's not me. When I'm barbecuing, I take it seriously and I don't drink alcohol. But I do enjoy a good adult beverage when I'm eating barbecue, when I'm celebrating a victory, or when I just need to kick back.

I started drinking the world's best booze, Crown Royal, when I was in my late twenties. Even back then, before I had worked a day in the world of food, I recognized the excellence of smooth blended whiskey. But then more of my friends started figuring it out, too. And before too long—this was still during my wilder days when I was going to a lot of parties and group gatherings—I would set that blue bag of Crown on a table, turn around for a second, and it would be gone. So it was during that time of my life that I also developed an appreciation for scotch. (When you set down a bottle of scotch in those days, you didn't have to worry about anybody else drinking it.) As I grew up and out of those partying days and started socializing in a moderate fashion, I came back to drinking what I love: Crown Royal. (Damn, I hope my agent is reading this, because Crown Royal ought to be paying me for this free commercial, don't you think?)

Real Southern Sweet Tea

If I'm working, which is to say I'm not drinking anything strong because I'm focused on winning a competition, I don't drink anything besides sweet tea. I love sweet tea, truly. It's the drink of the South, the drink of my home. Here's how we do it.

Makes 2 quarts

1 ounce (2 tablespoons) loose black tea
2 quarts room-temperature water
5 cups sugar

1 quart cold water
6 lemons, sliced

Bring 1 quart of water room-temperature to a boil in a saucepan. Pour the boiling water into a pitcher or large bowl, add the loose tea, and let steep for 5 to 10 minutes.

In the meantime, fill a large pitcher (large enough to hold at least 2 quarts of liquid) with the remaining 1 quart room-temperature water.

Strain the brewed tea into the pitcher containing the room-temperature water. Discard the tea leaves. Set the pitcher aside.

In a small nonreactive pot, combine the sugar and cold water. Bring to a boil over medium heat, stirring to dissolve the sugar. Add the lemons and remove from the heat. Allow to cool for 10 minutes. Strain the lemon-sugar syrup into the pitcher. Discard the lemon slices. Refrigerate the sweet tea until serving time.

Peachtree Crown Royal Cocktail

Anybody who's ever seen me on *Pitmasters* knows that Crown Royal is my drink of choice. Students who come to my classes bring me bottles; folks who come up to my rig at barbecue contests bring me bottles, too. I'm grateful, because after a long day of barbecuing I always relax with a little Crown and water—because every king can always use another Crown. But on occasion, I like to surprise my liver with something different. This is as Georgia of a drink as you can get, with a little help from our Canadian neighbors.

Makes 2 cocktails

1 quart cold water
2 ounces Crown Royal whiskey
2 ounces (¼ cup) peach schnapps
Splash of cherry syrup

4 ice cubes
2 quarters of a fresh ripe Georgia peach, peeled
2 fresh mint leaves

In a cocktail shaker or a large glass, combine the Crown Royal, schnapps, and syrup. Stir together. Place 2 ice cubes in each cocktail glass, and pour the mixture over the ice. Garnish each cocktail with a peach quarter and mint leaf.

Jenkins Punch

My granny always made this punch. She practically raised me; we lived with her until my daddy bought us a house and moved us out when I was still a little boy. My grandmother was a hardworking Southern woman, always cooking and cleaning her house. This is her recipe for as refreshing and fragrant a summer drink as you can imagine—a really intensely flavored version of sweet tea, if you will. It's a family favorite to this day. (It doesn't call for Crown Royal, and I don't even mind.) One thing, though: My granny's last name wasn't Jenkins, and she never did tell me who this recipe is originally named after; that's a mystery for the ages, I guess.

Serves 4

1 quart cold water
2 cups sugar
Grated zest of 3 lemons
Juice of 3 lemons

1 tablespoon almond extract
1 tablespoon vanilla extract
2 cups brewed tea, cooled

In a large pot, combine 1 quart cold water with the sugar and lemon zest. Bring to a boil, and let boil for 5 minutes. Then remove from the heat and let cool completely.

Add the lemon juice, the extracts, and the tea to the cooled liquid. Stir to mix well. Refrigerate.

Serve cold, over plenty of ice.

Banana Pudding

For some people in the South, dessert doesn't count unless it's one thing and one thing only: this one.

Serves 6 to 8

1½ cups sugar

1 14-ounce can sweetened evaporated milk

2 cups whole milk

4 eggs, separated (reserve egg whites for meringue, if using)

3 tablespoons all-purpose flour, sifted

½ 12-ounce box vanilla wafers (reserve a few for crumbled topping)

4 ripe bananas, thinly sliced

1 teaspoon cream of tartar (for meringue, if using)

In a medium saucepan over medium heat, combine the sugar and both milks. Stir until the sugar is completely dissolved. Turn the heat to low.

Add the egg yolks and flour to the pan. Stir until the mixture begins to thicken. Remove the pan from the heat and let the mixture cool.

In a large, clear ovenproof bowl or other serving dish, layer half of the cooled custard, then half of the vanilla wafers, then half of the bananas. Repeat the layers. Top with crumbled vanilla wafers. The pudding may also be topped with a meringue, if desired. Set the dish aside.

Preheat the oven to broil.

For the meringue:
Pour the reserved egg whites into a large mixing bowl. Using a handheld electric mixer, beat the egg whites with the cream of tartar until stiff peaks form. Top the pudding with this meringue. Place the bowl on a lower rack under the broiler and cook for 2 to 3 minutes, until the meringue browns. Remove the pudding from the oven and enjoy.

Apple Crunch

I'm known for barbecue, not for baking. But there are times when I'm called on to produce a dessert, and I'll tell you right now that there's nothing easier to make than this apple crunch. It's like apple pie without the hassle; you don't even have to make a crust. If you're really feeling desperate and in a big hurry, you can top the apples with half of the batter of a boxed cake mix; it's good that way, too.

Serves 6

4 cups peeled, cored, and sliced apples, preferably Granny Smith
¾ cup all-purpose flour
1 cup sugar
1 teaspoon ground cinnamon

½ teaspoon salt
8 tablespoons (1 stick) unsalted butter, cut into pieces, at room temperature, plus extra for the baking dish
Vanilla ice cream (optional)

Preheat the oven to 350°F.

Lightly butter a 9-inch square baking dish. Place the apple slices in the baking dish.

In the bowl of a food processor, combine the flour, sugar, cinnamon, and salt. Pulse a couple of times to combine. Add the butter and pulse until the mixture resembles coarse crumbs.

Sprinkle the crumb mixture over the apples.

Bake for 40 to 45 minutes, until the apples are tender. Serve warm, with ice cream, if you like.

Grilled Peaches with Apricot Glaze

When I thought about writing a cookbook, I didn't want to create one like many of the ones I saw on the market already—books that had a bunch of made-up barbecue recipes for things like grilled peaches. Then I realized that I actually *do* grill peaches in the summertime when I want a little something sweet for dessert! You can read other people's versions, but mine is the best. Tip: Make these when you're already smoking something in the smoker, so it's already hot and you can just lay them in there; don't make it hard for yourself.

If you are using wooden skewers, they must be soaked in water for at least 12 hours before using. If you have stainless steel or other metal skewers, soaking is not a concern.

Serves 4

4 fresh ripe Georgia peaches
8 tablespoons (1 stick) unsalted butter
1 cup (packed) dark brown sugar

1 ounce (2 tablespoons) dark rum
10 ounces (1¼ cups) apricot preserves
Vanilla ice cream (optional)

Heat a smoker to 325°F.

Pit the peaches and cut each one into quarters. Place the quarters on skewers. Lay the skewers on a large aluminum pan.

In a small saucepan over medium-low heat, combine the butter, brown sugar, rum, and preserves. Stir to thoroughly combine.

Glaze the peaches with the preserves mixture, place the pan in the smoker, and cook for 4 minutes on each side or until the peaches are soft. Serve the peaches atop vanilla ice cream, if you like.

"Barbecue is a simple food. Don't mess it up."

—MYRON MIXON

ACKNOWLEDGMENTS

From Myron Mixon:

I think I'm the greatest barbecue cook in the world—correction, I *know* I am the greatest barbecue cook in the world—but I'm humble in one key respect: I know I didn't get here without the love and support of my family. First and foremost among them is my wife, Faye, who is always by my side. She is my rock. Right behind her are my children: my daughter, Kylie, and my sons, David, Cory, and Michael. I'd also like to thank my mother, Gaye; my mother-in-law, Evelyn Goodroe; and my brothers, Tracy and Vince.

Man cannot live by other people alone, and I want to thank my loyal dogs, Jack, Lola, Bella, and Winston, for their unconditional love.

I would also like to thank John Markus, a world-class television writer and producer, for his passion for barbecue; Elmer Yoder for raising the best hogs, not to mention his dedication and respect for animal husbandry; and Jim and Jimmy Maxey for building smokers that help me win. I'd also like to thank Judy Ledford, Tony Woodard, Billy Steve Satterfield, Bonita Carr, David and Jon Hair, Nick Cochran, Wayne and Sandy Johnson, Edd Harris, Rhonda Lamb Heath, Suzanne Cooper, Angie Harpe, and Kenny Calhoun.

In putting together this book, I would like to thank Michael Psaltis, my agent and a tough fighter in his own right; Kelly Alexander, the best damn food writer in the business; Tom Rankin, an outstanding documentary photographer; Alex Martinez, of Alex Martinez Photography, for the striking and delicious food images; and Ryan Doherty, our editor at Random House, who recognized that my story needed telling, and the rest of his team of talented editors and designers who made this book a reality.

From Kelly Alexander:

The experience of walking a mile in another person's shoes is familiar to every writer, but the chance to do so in the boots of the formidable Myron Mixon is priceless. Many people want to know what The Man in Black is *really* like, and I'm here to tell you that he's a smarter and gentler man than the television cameras reveal and that I'm proud to call him a friend. I want to thank Myron and his family for their diligence, patience, and hospitality. I would also like to thank some of the food scholars and historians whose work about Southern food in particular informs this book, especially John Egerton, James Villas, Marcie Ferris, and the late Bill Neal. I would like to thank my mentor in the world of food, Colman Andrews, whose work inspires me most of all. I'd like to say that the culinary-literary super-agent Michael Psaltis is the ambassador of all good food writing. And I'd like to thank my family, especially my husband, Andrew, and my sons, Louis and Dylan, who sustain me.

Index

A

Aluminum foil and pans, 10

Apalachicola River System, 101

Appearance of food, 13, 48

Apple and Bacon–Stuffed Chicken Breasts, 42

Apple City Barbecue Team, 48

Apple Crunch, 156

Apple wood, 9

Apricot Glaze, Grilled Peaches with, 157

Apricot wood, 9

B

Baby back ribs, 69, 71–73

    recipe for, 79–80

Bacon and Apple-Stuffed Chicken Breasts, 42

Bacon-Wrapped Chicken Livers, 128, 129

Bacon-Wrapped Coca-Cola Chicken Breasts, 39

Baked beans, 111, 113

    recipe for, 114–115

Baked Potatoes, Barbecue Stuffed, 140

Banana pudding, 147–148

    recipe for, 155

Barbecue, history of, 8

Barbecue basics, 3–13

    appearance of food, 13, 48

    difference between grilling and barbecuing, 5–6

    fire starting, 12–13

    gas grills, 6–8

    kettle grills, 7, 8

    opening smokers, 6

    pantry essentials, 9–10

    rest times, 12

    taste of food, 4–5

    water pan in smoker, 11–12

    wood used, 8–9

Barbecue Chef Salad, 144

Barbecue Deviled Eggs, 125

Barbecue Nachos, 139

Barbecue Rub, Basic, 20

Barbecue Stuffed Baked Potatoes, 140

Barbecue Wings, 33

Basic Barbecue Rub, 20

Basic Chicken Rub, 20

Basic Hickory Sauce, 22, 23

Basic Vinegar Sauce, 22, 23

BBQ Pitmasters (television show), xx, 127, 151

Beard, James, 127

Beef, 86–99 (*see also* Brisket)

    Beef Injection and Marinade, 21

    Beef Ribs, 81–82

    Beef Rub, 20

    Beef Tenderloin, 97

    Burnt Brisket Ends, 91

    Myron Mixon's Prize-Winning Whistler Burger, 98–99

    Perfect Brisket, 90–91

    Perfect Porterhouse Steak, 95

    Prime Rib, 96

Beef broth concentrate, 10

Beef Injection and Marinade, 21

Beef ribs, 69

    recipe for, 81–82

Beef Rub, 20

Beverages (*see* Drinks)

Big Green Egg, 7

Big Pig Jig, Vienna, Georgia, xviii

Bogart, Humphrey, 147

Bologna, Smoked Jack, 61

Boston butt, 54, 57

Brisket, 87–88

    Burnt Brisket Ends, 91

    information on, 92–93

    Perfect Brisket, 90–91

Brunswick Stew, 122

Buffalo Wings, 32
Burgers
  grilling, 99
  Pork Burgers, 64
  Whistler Burgers, 64, 88, 98–99
Burnt Brisket Ends, 91

C

Cajun Louisiana hot sauce, 10
Canadian National Barbecue Championship, 88
Catfish, Fried, 131
Catfish-Shrimp Alfredo, 128, 134–135
Ceramic cookers, 7
Chadolbaegi, 87
Charcoal, 13, 93
Chef Salad, Barbecue, 144
Cherry wood, 9
Chicken, 24–45
  Apple and Bacon–Stuffed Chicken Breasts, 42
  Bacon-Wrapped Chicken Livers, 128, 129
  Bacon-Wrapped Coca-Cola Chicken Breasts, 39
  Barbecue Wings, 33
  Basic Chicken Rub, 20
  Buffalo Wings, 32
  Chicken Salad, 143
  Chicken Wings, 32–33
  competition category, 25–27
  cutting up, 37
  Myron Mixon's World-Famous Cupcake
    Chicken, 29–30
  Myron's Signature Buttermilk Fried Chicken, 45
  Old-Fashioned Barbecue Chicken, 31
  pulled chicken sandwiches, 40
  Sauce and Glaze, 23
  Whole Chicken, 40
  Wishbone Chicken, 31, 36–37
Chili powder, 45
Churchill, Sir Winston, 47
Coca-Cola Chicken Breasts, Bacon-Wrapped, 39
Coleslaw, 111
  recipe for, 119

Cookers (see Barbecue basics)
Cornbread, Cracklin', 120
Corned beef, 87
Cosby, Bill, 87
Country-style ribs, 72
Cracklin' Cornbread, 120
Cracklin' Skins, 60
Crown Royal, 148, 151
Cupcake chicken, 26–27, 29–30
Cutting up chicken, 37

D

Desserts, 147–148
  Apple Crunch, 156
  Banana Pudding, 155
  Grilled Peaches with Apricot Glaze, 157
Deviled Eggs, Barbecue, 125
Drinks, 147–152
  Jenkins Punch, 152
  Peachtree Crown Royal Cocktail, 151
  Real Southern Sweet Tea, 149

E

Eggs, Barbecue Deviled, 125

F

Fire, starting, 12–13
Fish and seafood, 100–109
  Catfish-Shrimp Alfredo, 128, 134–135
  Fried Catfish, 131
  Lobster, 105
  Lowcountry Boil, 133
  Mullet, 103
  Prawns, 108
  Salmon, 106
  Trout, 109
Flint River, 101
Florida BBQ Association, xv
Fried Catfish, 131
Fried Chicken, Myron's Signature Buttermilk, 45
Fruit woods, 8, 9, 47

G

Garnishes, 48
Gas grills, 6–8
Glazes, 15
    Chicken Sauce and Glaze, 23
    Grilled Peaches with Apricot Glaze, 157
    Hog Glaze, 23
Grapevine wood, 9
Grilled Peaches with Apricot Glaze, 157
Grilled Sausage, 62
Grilling
    burgers, 99
    difference between barbecuing and,
        5–6
Guthrie, Woody, 25

H

Half and Half solution, 59
Hamburgers (*see* Burgers)
Hickory Sauce, Basic, 22, 23
Hickory wood, 8
Hog, 46–67 (*see also* Pork)
    competition category, 48–49, 51
    Cracklin' Skins, 60
    Hog Glaze, 23
    Hog Injection, 21
    Hog Loins, 56
    Whole Hog, 53–55
Hors d'Oeuvres, Redneck Sausage, 63
Hot sauce, 10

I

Injections, 15, 16, 19
    Beef Injection and Marinade, 21
    Hog Injection, 21
    for whole hog, 54–55

J

Jack Daniel's World Championship Invitational
    Barbecue competition, xv
Jack's Old South Hickory Sauce, 10

Jack's Old South Team, xv, xvi, xvii
Jack's Old South Vinegar Sauce, 10, 23
Jenkins Punch, 152

K

Kale, as garnish, 48
Kansas City BBQ Society (KCBS) competitions,
    xv, 13, 51, 57, 70, 71
Kansas City-style ribs, 72
Kettle grills, 7, 8

L

Lamb
    Lamb Shoulder, 130
    Rack of Lamb, 85
Layered Salad with Potato Sticks, 121
Lightered knots, 17
Lighter fluid, 13, 93
Lobster, 105
Lock-&-Dam BBQ Contest, Augusta,
    Georgia, xix–xx
Loin back ribs, 72
Lowcountry Boil, 133

M

Mama's Slaw, 119
Marinades, 15, 19
    Beef Injection and Marinade, 21
    Rib Marinade, 21
Markus, John, xx
Meat Loaf, 136
Memphis in May (MIM) competitions, xv, 13, 48,
    51, 57, 61, 70, 71
Mills, Mike, 48
Minor's products, 10, 21
Mixon, Jack, xiii–xvi, xviii, 17, 47–48, 61,
    101–102
MSG (monosodium glutamate), 10
Mullet, 103
Myron Mixon's Prize-Winning Whistler Burger,
    98–99

Myron Mixon's World-Famous Cupcake Chicken, 29–30
Myron's Peach Baked Beans, 114–115
Myron's Signature Buttermilk Fried Chicken, 45

N
Nachos, Barbecue, 139
National Pork Board, 58

O
Oak wood, 8
Old-Fashioned Barbecue Chicken, 31
Open-pit cooking, 17, 19, 93
Ovid, 101

P
Pans, aluminum, 10
Pantry essentials, 9–10
Peach Baked Beans, Myron's, 114–115
Peaches, Grilled, with Apricot Glaze, 157
Peachtree Crown Royal Cocktail, 151
Peach wood, 9
Pear Salad, Stuffed, 123
Pear wood, 9
Pepper jack cheese, 61
Perfect Brisket, 90–91
Perfect Porterhouse Steak, 95
Pimiento Cheese, 145
Polish kielbasa-style sausage, 62
Pork (see also Hog)
    Pork Burgers, 64
    Pork Loin, 65
    pork ribs (see Ribs)
    Pork Shoulder, 57–58
    Redneck Sausage Hors d'Oeuvres, 63
    Sausage, 62–63
    Sausage-Stuffed Pork Chops, 84
    Stuffed Pork Tenderloin, 67
Pork lard, 45
Porterhouse Steak, Perfect, 95

Potatoes
    Barbecue Stuffed Baked Potatoes, 140
    Layered Salad with Potato Sticks, 121
    Potato Salad, 111, 116
Power cooking, 93
Prawns, 108
Prime Rib, 96
Pulled chicken sandwiches, 40

R
Real Southern Sweet Tea, 149
Recipes
    Apple and Bacon–Stuffed Chicken Breasts, 42
    Baby Back Ribs, 79–80
    Bacon-Wrapped Chicken Livers, 129
    Bacon-Wrapped Coca-Cola Chicken Breasts, 39
    Banana Pudding, 155
    Barbecue Chef Salad, 144
    Barbecue Deviled Eggs, 125
    Barbecue Nachos, 139
    Barbecue Stuffed Baked Potatoes, 140
    Barbecue Wings, 33
    Basic Barbecue Rub, 20
    Basic Chicken Rub, 20
    Basic Hickory Sauce, 22
    Basic Vinegar Sauce, 22, 23
    Beef Injection and Marinade, 21
    Beef Ribs, 81–82
    Beef Rub, 20
    Beef Tenderloin, 97
    Brunswick Stew, 122
    Buffalo Wings, 32
    Burnt Brisket Ends, 91
    Catfish-Shrimp Alfredo, 134–135
    Chicken Salad, 143
    Chicken Sauce and Glaze, 23
    Chicken Wings, 32–33
    Cracklin' Cornbread, 120
    Cracklin' Skins, 60
    Fried Catfish, 131
    Grilled Peaches with Apricot Glaze, 157

Recipes (*cont.*)

Hog Glaze, 23

Hog Injection, 21

Jenkins Punch, 152

Lamb Shoulder, 130

Layered Salad with Potato Sticks, 121

Lobster, 105

Lowcountry Boil, 133

Mama's Slaw, 119

Meat Loaf, 136

Mullet, 103

Myron Mixon's Prize-Winning Whistler
    Burger, 98–99

Myron Mixon's World-Famous Cupcake
    Chicken, 29–30

Myron's Peach Baked Beans, 114–115

Myron's Signature Buttermilk Fried Chicken, 45

Old-fashioned Barbecue Chicken, 31

Peachtree Crown Royal Cocktail, 151

Perfect Brisket, 90–91

Perfect Porterhouse Steak, 95

Pimiento Cheese, 145

Pork Burgers, 64

Pork Loin, 65

Pork Shoulder, 57–58

Prawns, 108

Prime Rib, 96

pulled chicken sandwiches, 40

Rack of Lamb, 85

Real Southern Sweet Tea, 149

Redneck Sausage Hors d'Oeuvres, 63

Rib Marinade, 21

Rib Spritz, 73

St. Louis Ribs, 76–77

Salmon, 106

Sausage, 62–63

Sausage-Stuffed Pork Chops, 84

Smoked Jack Bologna, 61

Smoked Turkey, 43

Stuffed Pear Salad, 123

Stuffed Pork Tenderloin, 67

Tangy Sweet Sauce, 23

Trout, 109

Whole Chicken, 40

Whole Hog, 53–55

Wishbone Chicken, 36–37

Zesty Potato Salad, 116

Redneck Sausage Hors d'Oeuvres, 63

Rest times, 12

Reynière, Alexandre Balthazar Laurent Grimod
    de la, 15

Rib Marinade, 21

Ribs, 69–85

    baby back ribs, 69, 71–73, 79–80

    beef, 69, 81–82

    buying guide, 72

    competition category, 70–71

    cooking tips, 72–73

    country-style, 72

    Kansas City-style, 72

    loin back, 72

    St. Louis, 69, 72, 76–77

    spareribs, 69, 72

    spritzing, 73

    types of, 69, 72

Rubs, 15, 16, 19

    Basic Barbecue Rub, 20

    Basic Chicken Rub, 20

    Beef Rub, 20

Rudner, Rita, 3

S

St. Louis ribs, 69, 72

    recipe for, 76–77

Salads

    Barbecue Chef Salad, 144

    Chicken Salad, 143

    Layered Salad with Potato Sticks, 121

    Stuffed Pear Salad, 123

Salmon, 106

Sandwiches
    Chicken Salad, 143
    Pimiento Cheese, 145
    pulled chicken, 40
Sauces, 15
    Basic Hickory Sauce, 22, 23
    Basic Vinegar Sauce, 22, 23
    Chicken Sauce and Glaze, 23
    Tangy Sweet Sauce, 23
Sauerbraten, 88
Sausage, 62–63
Sausage-Stuffed Pork Chops, 84
Seafood (*see* Fish and seafood)
Seasonings, 15
Shiners, 72
Shrimp
    Catfish-Shrimp Alfredo, 134–135
    Lowcountry Boil, 133
Side dishes, 110–125
    Barbecue Deviled Eggs, 125
    Barbecue Nachos, 139
    Barbecue Stuffed Baked Potatoes, 140
    Cracklin' Cornbread, 120
    Layered Salad with Potato Sticks, 121
    Mama's Slaw, 119
    Myron's Peach Baked Beans, 114–115
    Stuffed Pear Salad, 123
    Zesty Potato Salad, 116
Smoked Jack Bologna, 61
Smoked Turkey, 43
Smoke ring, 93
Smokers (*see* Barbecue basics)
Spareribs, 69, 72

Spices, 45
Spritzing ribs, 73
Stew, Brunswick, 122
Street, Paul, 98
Stuffed Pear Salad, 123

T
Tangy Sweet Sauce, 23
Taste of food, 4–5
Tea, Real Southern Sweet, 149
Tenderloin, Beef, 97
Trout, 109
Turkey, 43

V
Vinegar Sauce, Basic, 22, 23

W
Wagyu cattle, 92, 95
Water pan, in smoker, 11–12, 93
Webers, 7
Whistler Burgers, 64, 88, 98–99
Wishbone Chicken, 31, 36–37
Wood, 8–9
Woodard, Tony, xiv
Wright, Steven, 69

Y
Yoder, Elmer, 53
Yoder's Butcher Block, 53

Z
Zesty Potato Salad, 116

MYRON MIXON was quite literally born to barbecue. His father, Jack, owned a barbecue take-out business in Vienna, Georgia, which Myron helped run. His parents started selling Jack's Old South Barbecue Sauce, and after his father died in 1996, Myron thought that by entering competitions he could sell some sauce. He was hooked. He has appeared on the *Today* show, *The Tonight Show with Jay Leno,* and the *Late Late Show with Craig Ferguson.*

KELLY ALEXANDER is a former editor at *Saveur* and *Food & Wine* magazines, and her work has appeared in the *New York Times,* the *New York Times Magazine, Gourmet,* and *Newsweek,* among others. She also teaches food writing at Duke University and is a graduate of Northwestern University's Medill School of Journalism.